Not Only When the Rains Falls

Adventures in Awakening

Rita Reynolds

Published in 2018, by ROCKIT PRESS

ISBN: ISBN 978-0-9981719-1-3 Paperback

ISBN: 978-0-9981719-2-0 eBook

Library of Congress Control Number: 2018947422

Printed in the United States of America

Rockit Press

Dedicated to Michael, Tim, Anne, and Jake,
and all my friends, here and beyond
including Snowy, Calliope, Jonathan, Rosie and Christina,
with my greatest love, respect, and appreciation.

Acknowledgments

So many have made this book possible over the past six years. To those who are spoken of within the following pages, a deep bow of gratitude for offering so much light, inspiration, and opportunities for my own growth.

To those who encouraged and assisted in the actual work of the manuscript – you have been my support team throughout, my tireless editors and proofreaders, helping me understand how to speak with a clearer voice. And especially for your determination that I keep going despite those discouraging times known to all authors and care givers: Thank You! You are my personal helper-angels: Ron Wilson, Dianne Durant, Mary Jo Doig, TJ Banks, Pat Daly-Lipe, Anne Arringon, Sylvia Young, Mary Alice Santoro, Kay Pfaltz, Kyle Anne Gabbard-Alley, Bernie Siegel, and of course my sons, Michael and Tim Reynolds.

And a very special Thank You to Shauna Jackson of Rockit Press for her patience and most excellent publishing skills.

Finally, to my beloved angels, guides and ancestors of those "other" realms without whom nothing in my life and work would be possible.

Table of Contents

More Friends, Human and Otherwise

Teachers and Friends of Other Realms

Foreword

RITA'S BOOK *Not Only When The Rain Falls* is about the beauty and reverence for life we should all experience. Her stories can guide you to feel a reverence for all life. I have always felt nature has all the answers and tell people when they have a problem go out in nature and you will find your answer. A tree grows around a nail. A stream runs into an obstruction and makes beautiful sounds and finds a new way or a little pig raising a baby tiger when its mother dies. Our house was a zoo and I have written about it because it truly taught our family to have a reverence for life. Schweitzer and I have been picking up worms, washed by the rain onto the pavement, for decades and returning them to the earth.

I have also learned to be as smart and well behaved as my pet and to care for myself as well as I care for my animals. They all teach me to love life and show me how to survive when disease threatens their lives. Their names also make my day. We live with a Miracle and Hope, as well as, a little Dickens, Rags, Furphy and many more. I ask you all to read the poem *Rags* on the internet, about a dog named Rags, by Edmund Vance Cooke

In closing Miracle was named after a cat named Miracle who appeared in a lady's dream, and told her how to treat her cancer. She followed the advice and is alive and well today. Miracle was an incredible companion who feared nothing and acted more like a dog than a cat. So when there was a local dog show I entered her in it and told the people running things she thought she was a dog and I didn't want to disappoint her. Well all the dogs loved her and she rubbed noses with every one of them no matter how large or small they were and was the hit of the show. The following year the advertisement for the show read: "Dog Show for dogs only." I knew what they were telling me.

One day, Bobbie and I were partially dressed getting ready to go to the airport and couldn't find Miracle. So we were running around the house yelling "Miracle, Miracle" until Bobbie said, "What are the neighbors going to think?" So we stopped.

So read on and enter the world Rita is sharing with you.

Bernie Siegel, MD author of
*Love, Animals & Miracles; 365
Prescriptions For The Soul; and
Love, Medicine & Miracles.*

www.berniesiegelmd.com

Preface

How vital and urgent it seems to us to ask questions and seek the answers, to know the why, when and how of the intricate aspects of our lives, individual and collective. Why is life a fierce storm one moment, calm and clear the next? Why is there torture, pain, illness and cruelty in the world and how can we all live with peace and compassion? What is life for anyway? Why must there be separation by death or loss? We *need* to know – this desire and resulting search are what seem to drive most of us, human creatures that we are.

All of nature already knows those answers, they don't even have to question. Those of other realms and dimensions always know as well, understand everything in infinite intersecting patterns and vibrations. They know all, accept and integrate all. We humans, however, stand apart – from one another, from those of the natural world, from other realms, even from our true, inner selves.

These "others" are here for us, to help us heal in all the ways we hurt, to help us find the answers to all our questions. We just need to ask, and then to listen. I was born asking and I've never stopped. What follows is what I've learned along the way to help me listen, and how it has encouraged me in my own search for the peace and comfort I have longed for.

And so I offer the following stories for your consideration that they might be as guides and companions as you travel through your days. Each chapter was put to paper straight from inspiration that invariably flows without pause into my mind when I am focused elsewhere, perhaps washing dishes, cleaning the barn or picking out bananas at the store. And then suddenly there it is: one word, a title, or a complete thought announcing, *Here I am! Write me down, share me with the world.* And, being intrigued, I have complied again and again as the inspiration has poured in for over four years. You are holding the result in your hands.

There is no planned sequential order to the chapters and there is reason for that. This book is meant to be opened at random when you need a question answered or to seek comfort and direction. Maybe you're sad and could use a little perspective on things, to know you are not the only one going through such a difficult time. Your intuition, always with you, will guide you to what you need to read. Of course, you can start with page one if you wish – there are no rules here! And that's one of the purposes of this project – to help in any way possible.

To offer a bit of structure, the book is divided into three sections presenting those who have – and continue to be – my dearest, most profound teachers and friends, beginning with all of the natural world, then human beings and what I categorize as "others", such as a chair, or stone, even a thunderstorm. Since I was a small child angels and spirit guides have cared for and about me, very evident even though mostly unseen, so they, too, have a voice here. They have been my companions who have protected me at times of high danger, *gently* scolded me when I have asked for their advice and then ignore it, or when I have made a judgment of another in error (they do not believe in judging others!)

Often they will send me dreams to ponder on and learn from, dreams I remember clearly for decades. They recognize and make allowances for my humanness, never leave me, and above all, love me without condition.

My adventures, experiences, questions and insights are the connecting threads that weave together this story. All of those written about here, as well as myself and you, our reader, are part of an amazing team. Is our collective purpose as that team, to bring to human consciousness the vastly important role of un-bounded Love and a reverence for life itself? I deeply believe so.

So I hope you enjoy what is within these pages and find helpful, reliable friends among the words. They may appear as two-dimensional print upon page, but in truth they are open windows into another way of seeing, knowing, and discovering. Welcome to the adventure!

Rita M. Reynolds
Batesville, Virginia

*The Natural World
as Friend and Teacher*

Always Remember to Dance

LILLIE LOOKS UP AT ME with bright, questioning eyes. *Is it time to eat yet? Can I go out now? Will you fix my bed for me?* When I look down at her and smile she wags her tail, tentatively at first, then with assurance that I will, indeed, show up for her. She finally realizes she is safe and this is home. She picks up her squeaky toy and tosses it happily about, confident in her place here.

It wasn't always so for her. In 2005 she was a battered, bruised little Shih Tzu, found shivering alongside a highway in Ohio. Was she a rejected puppy mill dog? Had she been thrown from a car? Had she been beaten? No one will know for sure, only that this dog, probably only a year old, was alone, terrified, and defensive. So much so, the rescue group who took her began to feel that euthanasia might be the only option for this confused and reactive creature. No one could approach her, no one really wanted to. When she backed up and snarled at everyone and anything, there seemed little hope that she would ever have a happy life or find an accepting home and family.

But there is always hope. And there are people who throw caution out the window and say, "Why not try?" And so Lillie landed here, amidst my human family who thought I had lost my mind. The rescue group, relieved to have found one last chance for this troubled little soul, sent her bed, toys and food and a note that simply said, *Good Luck, and Thank You!* She has turned out to be delightful.

Sometimes we can wake up in the morning and wonder if Earth will survive. One scandal after another, disaster here, new deadly virus outbreak there. What now? Where is global unity and peace? What? Say that again? *There is no hope, we are doomed.*

Not so. There is always hope. We have to try, so we get up out of our beds each morning, put weary feet to floor, and trudge forward into the day, knowing deep within ourselves what seems unfixable always evolves, always eventually finds its way back to Centerpoint, balance, the natural order of things. Could this just be cosmic law?

Like the robins for example. The winter of 2014 took us deep into what was called, without affection, The Polar Vortex. Here in Virginia temperatures charged downhill to minus 15 with the wind chill factor. Without it, we reached zero. For nearly three days the arctic air mass held us tight, driving up fuel bills, driving down bravado.

But on January 12th the robins arrived. They perched along fences, hopped along the ground, chirping. Hope. It comes with the declaration in feathers and fortitude that yes, indeed, spring will come.

It's not often that we really give up hope. Is hope written into our DNA? Yes, life can get quite menacing and certainly grief alone over an impending loss can trigger deeply unsettled feelings of not making it back from the edge. We've all been there, and we will be again. Natural disasters, wars, illness, abuse and neglect... there are so many obstacles to our having hope. But it's always there... in the tiny seed deep in the cold, dark soil. In the sunset after a day's torrential rain; in the fledglings born high in a sturdy nest; in the earthworm that turns and aerates the soil so new plants may thrive; in the decaying tree trunk in the forest, nourishing the top soil; to the song of the first bird to awaken in the morning light.

Lillie has taught me much about hope. About the courage to see beyond even the most terrifying and confusing chatter that my mind may yell at me, blind-sighting me to what *can be*: the opposite of no-hope to yes, it really is going to be much, much better. All the signs are there; Lillie's upturned face tells me so.

Lillie still has boundary issues. But even so, we have made so much progress – based on hope and determination – that it's hard to remember that such a frightened, defensive, snarly heap of confused dog had just escaped from death row in Ohio. The rescue group who first took her in had tried so hard to work with her, but she was failing the necessary categories that would get her adopted, such as Friendly; Loves people; Plays well with others and even at her young age she was not going to give an inch. And so she was slated for euthanasia; just about everyone had given up on her.

But not my good friend, Vickie. Spotting her on the rescue's web site, she called me. "What do you think, Rita," she asked hopefully. "Would you be interested in working with her?" Fools rush in where angels…. "Sure!" I replied. After all, she would be what some of my friends consider a "Rita Dog" – one in the final throes of desperation.

Vickie, selfless, loving, wonderful Vickie, drove the little snarly dog from her home near Dayton, across the mountains of West Virginia and Virginia to my door. While not much seems to faze my friend, she did seem a bit pale when she arrived. The little dog, even more confused, backed herself into a corner in the kitchen, reared back, and yelled at everyone who came near her. My current dog family looked to me with anxiety, my human family shook their heads and rolled their eyes, and I, admittedly, wondered what I had gotten myself into.

The little frantic dog had been given the name Hildy by the rescue group. I wondered about that, Hildegaard? I looked it up. It meant "Warrior." That would not do, she needed a quiet, easy name. Yes, she was ready to fight, but stubborn Irish that I am, I *knew* I could change that. Her name became Lillie, after my great grandmother who was everything wonderful.

Vickie returned to Ohio, and the Reynolds family, two and four footed, settled in to figure out this strange, distant little creature who defended her bed and toys in the kitchen with all the rage of a lion. Most appropriate as in China, country of origin for her breed, Shih Tzu are known as Lion Dogs, and Guardians of the Gate. And guard her gate, this fierce little ball of white and gold fur, was determined to do. And, we all paid attention. Everyone tiptoed around her. She ruled, and she knew it.

Somewhere around the fifth day after she had taken up residence – and claimed her power over us – I decided no matter the consequences, I had to vacuum the floors. It was way overdue, but I had not wanted to frighten her with the noise. But, push comes to shove, out came the vacuum and with one eye on my little warrior, I started up the screeching machine. And Lillie came to life.

Leaping in joyous circles, her long, silken tail twirling behind her, she began to dance around and around while I pushed and pulled. Back and forth we went, me cleaning, she dancing. I finished and the vacuum fell silent. Still she looked expectant and for the first time since arriving, truly happy.

We cleaned the floors all over again. It was a glorious time.

Years have passed, ten as of this writing, and Lillie is a different dog. I can pick her up and hug her, give her a bath and brush out her magnificent tail. Donna, who grooms at the Animal Hospital, clips her coat and while Lillie has a *Caution – can be grumpy* sticker on her chart, she has gotten to be quite well behaved. As Donna will kindly tell me, "Lillie was good for us." Words never sounded so fine to me.

Lillie rarely snarls now, only if she feels her space is being invaded. She still has night terrors, rising violently from sleep to twist and yell, perhaps caused by old memories of previous abuse before she was found shivering and bruised by her rescuers.

But one habit Lillie has never lost – her love for the vacuum and her immediate fling into a joyous dance when it comes to life. I can say, "Lillie, do you want to help vacuum?" and she is instantly alert and on her feet, toes barely touching the ground as she flies toward me. She knows where I keep the vacuum, and runs to the closet, anticipating what is to come. And just today, I only *thought*: "Maybe I should vacuum" and she was off her bed and with eyes bright and shiny, leaping toward me. I choose to believe it is the love between us that allows such a connection.

Lillie will always have her boundaries, she will never play with the other dogs, she is very much her own dog, and she likes it that way. Routine is vital to her contentment and knowing her bed is her safe spot, hers alone, and that it will always be exactly where she expects it to be. And there is certainly nothing wrong with any of that. Likewise, she is gentle and sweet now, finally trusting that she really is home to stay, a home and family that respects and honors her just for who she is.

And when my own attitude gets low, my little warrior, bright soul that she is, reminds me it's time to haul out the vacuum and remember to dance.

Not Only When the Rain Falls

AN ENORMOUS PUDDLE STANDS IN the middle of the donkeys' upper pasture, the result of five inches of rain over the last two days. It reflects the trees that hang over it, clouds moving overhead, and a flock of small birds heading west. The puddle holds the present, but it also holds the past, good memory of a time when I had ducks in my family and they taught me about always being joyful.

White Pekins, Khaki Campbells, even a visiting small wild Mallard, for years found unrestrained delight whenever there was a sizeable rain and puddles would form in the fields and lawns. Chattering like children on a field trip, running with their wings extended my ducks would rush from puddle to puddle, swimming in circles, diving (if the puddle was deep enough) and drilling with their bills in the mud, creating a lovely gurgling sound as they searched for bugs and other forage. A rainy day was a spectacular day according to my ducks.

Ducks are amazing creatures ecstasy seems to come easily for them, whatever the moment brings (as long as they are safe, that is) they see as worthy of celebration, a great deal of conversation, and dancing up on their webbed feet with wings outstretched as if embracing the world in which they find themselves.

So it was not only when the rain fell, but at all times – a sunny day meant stretching out in the grass, necks extended, eyes closed, letting the warm rays penetrate their feathers. A cloudy day usually brought earthworms to the surface and that meant a feast – scurrying about, gathering and swallowing the worms, sharing their find with their friends of the feather. On hot days, the ducks found the cool darkness of thick weeds and settled in – no complaints, just acceptance. And sometimes, for no particular or obvious reason, they simply took off running across the grass as if completely thrilled just to be alive.

Five inches of rain in two days is quite a bit. I realize with climate change and global warming that amount is no longer considered extraordinary. And I have done what I could to keep a dry basement in the house and stalls in the barn. Outside drains are kept open and channels dug to re-route the gushes of water and the hay bales are buttoned down with tarps to keep them dry. Everything practical is done – except I that have forgotten to play in the rain. I have been so focused on being responsible, I have neglected one of the most important responsibilities of all: to find and wade right into the great gift of life. And few things offer that potential for joy than a massive, just freshly formed rain puddle eager for visitors.

My ducks have been gone for years and they are greatly missed. Now wild birds come to the puddles to dip in their beaks and take lovely, splashy baths there, flinging the water where it catches the light and shimmers midair. I believe *this* puddle calls to me right now.

I stand by this new and wondrous puddle and can almost see my old friends frolicking in its midst and I laugh for the remembrance. I slosh right into the middle of it and watch the mud squish out from under the soles of my boots, forming interesting patterns as it rises to the water's surface.

My ducks – my feathered gurus – just by being themselves, showed me how easy it is to find the upside to just about everything in life, how to be totally thrilled with whatever the day may bring. For a duck, *anything* in life is just like a huge, lovely, inviting puddle and those are the best – but being thrilled with life is for all times, not only when the rain falls.

Mo and the Mouse

TOMORROW IS THE FIRST OF October and it certainly is fall of the year. Trees are beginning to change color and drop their leaves. Cooler air has arrived, and this morning a young field mouse squeezed through some secret opening in the outside wall and emerged into the kitchen. Mo pounced, the mouse cried, and I leapt. Grabbing up my startled tiger cat clutching a terrified rodent, I took the two steps out the back door, opened Mo's mouth, and the tiny mouse, apparently physically none the worse for the event, fled at high speed for safety. I carried Mo back inside and placed him on the floor. I mentioned that collecting mice in the house was an excellent idea, hurting them was not. He looked at me, I looked at him and we each, then, went our separate ways. The time lapse? Perhaps 30 seconds. The incident was complete and Mo retired to his favorite chair for a nap. As the famous line from the Simpsons TV show goes, "Done is done."

So simple. Could I do the same?

You see, Mo versus Mouse had me reconsidering some uncomfortable, distressing events and people in my own life, not just recent ones, but also the odd few dating back years, even decades. Most of them long since finished and supposedly "done", why was I still dragging them along behind me like boulders, doing mental and emotional battle within myself? Why did I clutch them with such ferocity like prey while in effect, my refusal to move on was, instead, bound to consume *me*?

Outside the trees release their leaves this time of year without regret or fear, anger or self-pity, allowing newly forming buds to emerge for next spring's awakening. How would those new buds bring new leaves if the tree hung on to the old ones? Made sense to me. Yet, why was it so difficult for me to do the same? I thought of all the so-called spiritual platitudes: *Just forgive and forget; you have to let go of the past; give it all to God; just change your thinking.*

Okay. Tried them all, nothing works, not for me anyway. But I believe what might work for me is looking to the natural world I love and admire so much and where without fail I have found my greatest teachers: dogs and donkeys, landforms, the water cycle, seasons, night into day into night, gardens and forests, wild creatures, wind, clouds, an infamous cow, and – my lovely cat, Mo.

The list, of course, is endless – but there is one basic thing all such diversified form has in common. Some people call it living in the moment, but there is more to it than that. It's about flow – moving seamlessly and unencumbered by mental, emotional, even physical baggage. Not long ago a Black snake, easily six feet long, shed his skin along the bark of the maple tree in the front yard. It was impressive. I doubt the snake looked back, or thought about keeping part of the old skin for memory's sake, or questioned the wisdom of shedding his skin at all. By some magnificent, mysterious inner prompting, that snake knew the what, how, and when of wriggling out of that no longer useful skin, and not looking back, to simply continue on his way.

I seriously doubt those of the natural world see themselves

as criminals (predators) or victims (prey). Animals behave accordingly by intuition and instinct, but don't stand around and ponder their position on the food chain. We put those labels out there and assign other beings to them as we see them. It really is all a matter of human opinion. I admit I am really good at seeing myself as a victim, entitled to my outrage and anger, or my fear and regret. But these are categories, and as such keep me walled away from the inner intuitive flow that would allow me to move ahead unencumbered in life by such unnecessary and possibly harmful attitudes, with ease of mind and openness of heart.

So what if I had not been right there in the kitchen when Mo caught the field mouse who was, presumably, simply looking for a warm, safe place to spend the winter? What if Mo had killed and eaten the little critter? Would Mo have been "bad" for his thought to catch, and action to consume another living creature? Would the mouse have been "foolish" or "stupid" to have wandered into a house with cats? Or, would Mo have been doing his duty as Cat in eliminating the "invader" mouse? You can see how a person could view, label, and perhaps justify such a simple act of nature…and spend an awful lot of time and energy in the process.

But here's another take on the Mo and the Mouse incident. It's cooling down outside; mice, like many animals, birds, and bugs, instinctively know for their survival they need to fly south, hibernate, or seek shelter for the winter months. After all, some folks go to Florida for the coldest parts of the year. There is nothing "right" or "wrong" with any of that.

Mo, being Cat, chases things that move – a leaf, a dust bunny, a mouse. And, there is nothing "right" or "wrong" with that. All of it is simply inner promptings, being part of the flow of life. Had Mo killed the mouse, the essence of the mouse would have moved on to other worlds, other dimensions. I really doubt she would have been wringing her little etheric paws in regret or yelled "Unfair!" or cursed the cat. Like the snake shedding his skin, she would have simply wriggled out of her body and moved on with her journey.

I know I still have a lot of shedding to do, and new incidents and people further down the road of my life will want to stick like Carpenter's Glue to my brain. But from now on when I feel the need to curse or blame another, or pity myself for whatever excuse I invent, I am going to think of Mo curled up in his chair, the mouse off looking for seeds, and the Black snake, long since done with his old skin, busy finding a place to sleep for the coming months. If such a flowing existence works for the world of nature, I suspect there has to be something to it.

Every Day Can Be
That First Tomato....

...THE FIRST FRUIT OF THE summer garden: ripe, fragrant, sweet – deep red or brilliant yellow, Big Boy or Heirloom, I stand in the garden and absorb the sun's warmth into my pores as it comes off the vine and lands so full and gently in my hands.

Every dedicated gardener waits so long for that tomato! When the winds of winter whip across the bare and frozen ground; then first green shoots of spring poke bravely through the leaf mold. When garden beds are tilled and turned and renewed with compost. Then with a blessing, prayer, and tender love, tiny new plants are placed in carefully laid out rows. To reach that first tomato requires one's full and active participation, back-straining work tossed with the desire to nourish and support these beings given to our care, and patience as the plants move upward toward the light, their pace their own. No less is it the culmination of good cooperation between human strength, soil, water and light: pure energy of atoms and molecules. What a team!

How delicious the first bite of that vine-ripened orb – at initial harvest time there is a collective sigh that rises from those fortunate enough to taste the season's freshness. And while to city folk it may seem a silly pleasure, it so much more than that.

It is a celebration of life come to fruition, bringing with it into the present moment the whole amazing package of anticipation, nurturing, integration, and appreciation.

Holding now this first gift of the garden in my hands I recall how I awoke this morning, frightened over certain aspects of my life. *Oh no!* I yelled deep in my brain, *how will I ever manage?* And as I put my feet to the floor still so self-absorbed, there they were, watching me: Snowy, Jonathan, Lillie and Calliope, sweet loyal dogs always so happy to see me. Emma, on the stairs, purred for her breakfast. Stars bowed out before first light just crossing the mountains, and the wind stirred the wind chimes on the front porch. *This* moment, this venturing step into a new day, untangling from my frantic brain, became instead sweet and inviting, all its possibility asking for me to take it gently in my hands.

So why not *every* day, each one the harvest of all I have experienced, worked so hard for, tended to, cared about, seeds of one kind or another I have planted along the way, those I will always love in every bit of my soul: how perfectly is every day my "first tomato".

The Anything-is-Possible-Club
(and more about Lillie)

OCCASIONALLY, IT SEEMS TO BE a good idea to simply erase the presumed boundary between what we think is real and what is "merely" in our imagination. Lillie, always a contemplative, yet cautious little creature, decided one day that her stuffed duck was actually, quite possibly, a friend, someone not only to toss around, but to have conversation with, share thoughts, dreams, perhaps even her dinner. And while the little duck was not particularly interested in her food, there did seem to be a comradery between them – and as practical as I tend to be, I could feel the energy between them. Allowing her duck into her personal space was a big step for Lillie, always a bit of a loner struggling emotionally to allow herself to trust anyone. The duck won her over and now Lillie is much more at ease with the rest of us. But the little stuffed duck remains her best bud. I understand that they have started a club – the *Anything is Possible Club If You Believe.* Membership is free, should you wish to join.

Instinctive Curves:
Exercise of a Different Kind

A POPULAR FITNESS FRANCHISE CALLED Curves offers support-
ive ways for women to improve their health and stamina, hopefully leading to a long and vigorous life. I've never joined, although I have been tempted. But I figured putting in eight hours
of farm and small critter work a day should give me enough of a
workout. So I stay home, clean stalls, haul water, pitch hay and
otherwise tend to my large and small four-footed friends.

One form of *mind* exercise my home and farm work provides
that I don't believe a fitness club does, is to keep me constantly
alert to changes that can completely alter how I thought my day
was going to proceed. A willingness to adapt in at a second's notice is definitely part of my job description and an excellent way
to sharpen mental acuity. If I have to make plans in advance, for
example a doctor's appointment or lunch with friends, I have to
give my famous disclaimer: "I may have to change this at the last
minute...." People who know me are very forgiving.

Being malleable must be the appropriate approach to life because
everything in nature does change and adaptability so well. Since
the natural world has been functioning in good order far longer

than human beings have, I like to look to how nature solves its problems, even the small glitches. For example, I've noticed that in the natural world there doesn't seem to be much, if any, complaining just because one's day isn't going as planned. Plants and trees are good teachers for this kind of mental and emotional exercise that asks us to switch gears without giving up hope or losing our inner balance.

In the donkeys' pasture near the barn, are two young paradise trees. A prolific and fast growing species, paradise trees tend to spring up overnight in the strangest of places. One sprouted right next to the north, or shady side of the back of the barn. Obviously not getting the light it needs, its thin trunk stretches far out and then way up in a smooth curve reminiscent of half of a giant cup. In less than a year its small canopy of leaves is now able to gather all the sunlight it requires to thrive.

A short distance away, another paradise tree decided to take root right against the back wall of the old hen house. Up it went, doing what trees do so well, going straight toward the sky. That was two years ago. Last year, the youngster came up against one of those small roadblocks in life: the roof overhang. Undaunted, and as far as I could tell without complaining or placing blame, it simply began to curve slightly outward, just enough to clear the roof line, and then continue its straight and sunward climb.

This spring we talked about taking down the old henhouse and replacing it with a more efficient storage building. But we changed our plan, adapted, as it were, because we couldn't even think of dishonoring the tree's desire, against all glitches to, hopefully, live a long and vigorous life. I guess you could say we applauded its instinctual decision to keep on keeping on. The new building will just have to be built someplace else.

And a good thing we changed our plan because in April this year three baby squirrels, parked there by their mother (squirrel day care?), ran happily around the inside of the hen house, safe from hawks and other predators until they were big enough to be out on their own.

Everything's Right About Treats

THE DONKEYS HAD BEEN OUT in their pasture for their allotted time. Due to Julia's foot problems, they are only allowed three hours of grass grazing a day. But they want more. And we have two ways to deal with the process of returning – unwillingly – to the barn. Both ways involve treats.

Donkeys are pretty stubborn to begin with, and they sure can live up to their reputation. If things aren't going their way, they will push, kick or bite me. But they are also sweet and gentle, attuned to my moods. When I am sad or worried, they will not hesitate to nuzzle me with their soft noses, or lean gently against me in comradery. I'm the same way, sensitive to another's sorrow, but also stubborn if frustrated, although rather than kicking or biting, I will mope and feel abused. I don't recommend any of these negative ways of expression.

With donkeys – and with some folks (myself included) sometimes a quick declaration of what is needed, is called for. Getting behind my "girls" and clapping my hands usually sends them in the proper direction. If I am in a rut I can't get myself out of, someone saying "Get a grip, Rita!" works for me. One might call it a reality check.

But the second way to move donkeys and mopey folk is with

the promise of treats. I cannot over-emphasize the excellence of such a tool. And, a tool a treat truly is.

Donkeys are particularly fond of shredded carrots and sliced apples. I can usually get their attention simply by saying the words *Apple?* or, *Carrots?* And two heads rise from the grass, long ears pointing toward me, noses aquiver. And like happy pups they are hiking into the barn behind me. Treats are served, I thank them for their cooperative natures, and close the barn door.

Mission accomplished without bruises or bite marks, making it a good day for all involved.

Of course, we humans, being the (supposedly) more intelligent species, (supposedly) know that we just do what needs to be done and treats are not part of the equation. Go to work; get the task done; suffer the long hours, lack of appreciation by co-workers, employers, family, friends, politicians, corporate America.... *Just do it and shut up. Get through the day. Don't feel sorry for yourself.* Or as my grandfather used to say to his eldest daughter, my mother: *Be a good little soldier and pull yourself up by your bootstraps.*

Any of that sound sadly familiar?

But here's the truth: treats work just as well for us as for my donkeys, dogs, cats and all the variety of species who have roamed this property for nearly 40 years. Treats don't spoil anyone. They comfort, encourage, brighten a mood, help someone to feel special. After all, a treat is a gift given by someone who cares, or they would be mean to you rather than kind. Mean people don't give out treats.

So when I am in the midst of anything that requires difficulty on my part; or I'm stressed over a severe storm hitting us; or financial woes; or in pain – physical or emotional, I step away from the situation – if only for a moment - and think of a way to give myself a treat. The ways and means are endless, fun to conjure up, something to look forward to with delight when the opportunity appears.

A bit of that fresh blueberry pie in the fridge after morning chores. Thirty minutes with a cup of afternoon tea or coffee and a good book before beginning evening work. Time in the garden after paying bills. Ten minutes sitting outside on the porch steps – listening to the birds, admiring the mountain. A thirty minute nap with Snowy. A square of dark chocolate; one cookie.

There is nothing wrong with a treat. In fact, there is everything *right* with a treat. If you don't believe me, just ask my donkeys.

Rosie to the Core

Rosie always knew she was a Rottweiler at heart. Weighing in at only eight pounds and small enough to tuck under my arm, Rosie nonetheless knew that no intruder daring to cross the threshold stood a chance against her determined attacks upon their – okay, just the ankles, but oh could she inflict pain. No one would get past her self-proclaimed devotion to home and family. And while some insensitive people would rudely remark that she was "not a nice dog," or "What a mean dog," in truth Rosie was only doing what dogs have done down through history, guard and protect those she loved. She did have a soft side to visitors as well: once placed in their lap, she would fall asleep, snuggling happily into their arms.

Rosie is gone now, she crossed the famous Bridge of Many Colors in late October, 2013. And, she is greatly missed. Visitors arriving at the door are ushered in with pleasantries and offers of lunch. No little Yorkie/Cairn lunges at them, barking hysterically and snapping her remaining two teeth. There is no fierce warrior looking up at me, eyes proclaiming "Not to worry, Rita, I've got your back here."

But this she taught me: Even when I am having one of those days when I feel really small and insignificant, if I look inside, I'm oh so brave, very, *very* brave, and very BIG – a lion or lioness perhaps, a grizzly bear, a fire-breathing dragon or even a Rottweiler. But I'd rather think I'm a "Rosie" to the core, fierce, courageous, and loyal, but with a tender soul.

Forgiveness, by Rosie
(More about Rosie)

SOMETIMES IT'S GOOD TO GIVE up certain things, just to lighten the load we carry.

A person with whom I had a business relationship had, I felt, betrayed me. A signed contract had been broken repeatedly, promises made were not kept, and most of the large financial investment I had put in at the beginning of our work together was now lost. Furthermore, when I approached this person for compensation, I was ignored. I was angry, bitter, deeply concerned for the monetary loss and sad for the demise of what I had felt sure would be a successful endeavor. But far more destructive was the fact that it seemed the longer I carried the negative feelings and thoughts, the heavier everything in my life seemed to become.

I spoke to a few close friends of the circumstances and they were all sympathetic, agreeing that I had "been done wrong" and deserved better. And as much as I appreciated their allegiance, what I probably needed to hear was a gentle reprimand to stop pitying myself and look at the situation from a different perspective rather than the myopic one of being a victim suffering so much loss.

This is not an easy thing to do, nor does it provide a quick fix to material or monetary loss, let alone one's pride. Feelings of betrayal, especially, can be Velcro to the ego. Since I tend to take a jaundiced eye to any *human* person giving me advice, what did finally work for me was, in fact, the unspoken, unwavering wisdom from one those friends of fur and paw, my dogs.

Enlightenment came quite by accident – by my not looking where I was going and tripping over Rosie, who, being the color of the floor and determined to follow my every footstep, was too easy to miss as I rush around in my multiple chores. I am ashamed to say that this particular accidental trodding-on-dog was not the first time, and perhaps the biggest lesson I can learn is mindfulness: slowing down and paying attention. Since I am nowhere proficient at this valuable practice, I will probably tread on many more of my beloved little creatures in the future.

However, at the time in question, when I stepped on Rosie's paw she did her pitiful yelp, stood back, and looked up at me with bright little eyes, her nub of a tail wagging as hard as it could. I, full of apologies and guilt, picked her up and held her close vowing to never step on her paw again. Whether she simply took my word for it, or was thinking *Okay, sure, but when you do step on my paw again, it's ok,* I will never know, since I don't speak fluent "dog". But the bottom line from her and all the animals in my family over many years was – and always will be – the same: *Injury happened, it hurt, when's dinner?* And translated into eternal wisdom as: *Ouch!! Okay, I'm over it; life goes on. And regarding our friendship: we're good.*

Somehow, this particular time I got the message and realized its value if applied to other areas of my life. After an awful lot more apologies, hugs, and a few treats (guilt is a tough one, too) I put Rosie back down on the floor, stepped *around* her and went upstairs to my computer. What I then proceeded to do not only felt absolutely without question or hesitation, appropriate, but really good in my soul. I sent an email to my business associate, thanking her for one really good thing that had recently happened in our association and offering assistance if needed. My email ended on a cheerful note. As I hit the "send" key I felt a heaviness lift off of me and happily noted that every bit of my anger, resentment, self-pity and victimization was gone. Giving it all up had been that easy after all, thanks to my sweet, forgiving, onward marching little dog with tender paws.

The Sweet Potato Potential

THE REMAINING CROP OF LAST year's sweet potatoes sat clustered together in a basket in the kitchen. With the new crop joyously taking over this year's garden, it seemed advisable to sort through the basket and discard any potatoes that were ready for compost.

Near the top was a long, wrinkled, mostly dried tuber. While long past edible, it alone among its fellow potatoes had sent up a series of long, thin, most anemic looking shoots that had nearly invisible miniscule leaves clinging to the stems. I set the potato aside for compost and continued sorting.

Something kept pulling my attention back to it, however, and now finished with my task I placed it on the counter for further evaluation. What was it saying to me? I could almost make out the whisper in my mind, but my heart felt the usual tenderness when it is time for me to rescue someone in need. In need of what? In this case, I just did not know.

Michael wandered through the kitchen right at that moment (isn't it always the "right" moment?) and studying the strange sweet potato, remarked:

"Why don't you cut off the sprouted end and plant it in the garden?"

What? We had a jungle of vines from nine new plants, hardly space for yet another. Instead I found a large flower pot on the kitchen deck, filled it with fresh soil and carefully set the cut end down so that the spindly pale sprouts stood upright in their new-found sunlight. A good watering, many encouraging words, and I left the plant to its own journey.

Within a week new, vibrant green leaves filled the pot. Within two weeks the leaves now spilled over the edge, vines charging with typical sweet potato vigor across the deck, the sidewalk to the back door, and who knows to where from there.

When I sit beside my rescued friend, I feel three messages come clearly to me: *Thank you! Yes! I can do it!* and, *Look at me go!*

This all has happened in a rather difficult spot in my life and there have been many moments when I felt my own spirit to be pale and too thin to hold up the rest of me. So for this audacious potato that is oh, so sweet just for being who it is, I have three messages:

Thank you! If you can do it, so can I! and: *Look at me go!*

The Reluctant Fledgling

THESE HAD BEEN CHALLENGING WEEKS for me: the loss of two long-time animal companions, a torn muscle in my right arm, and a host of discouraging news. Somewhere in this time I walked into my barn and looked up, a recent and frequent habit of mine, to check on the latest nest of fledgling barn swallows. To my delight I found three fat, fuzzy bodies perched precariously on various rafters, with the fourth fledgling still in the nest, looking anxious.

"Congratulations!" I called (but not to scare them), cheering them on as they entered their next great adventure. Being born scarcely two weeks earlier was exciting enough, then on wobbly wings making it out of the nest. Now they were preparing to venture forth into the world. I was thrilled for them – having witnessed this break-through event many times with countless new barn swallows over the years my family and I have lived here.

I turned my attention to the little guy peering down at me from over the edge of the nest. I could almost hear him say, *"Oh dear, oh dear, oh dear."* Amply large enough to be out with his siblings, I knew he just lacked the bravado that would launch him from the safety of his first home. And, from all those years of watching such an event, I knew he would quite soon find his courage, spread his wings and go.

It occurs to me that there is real wisdom in knowing just when to take flight, to pull away from whatever nest holds us be it physical, mental, emotional, even spiritual. Sometimes, it's just time to leave that space, once so safe and comforting. Initially, we don't want to, but we must in order to find new perches from which to gain different perspectives, or clear, boundless space to see how high and far we can go. Right then, like that last fledgling I, too, found myself saying *Oh dear, oh dear, oh dear* as I struggled to emotionally pull myself up far enough from my sadness to see new possibilities, let alone stretch and try my wings in new directions.

But I know from tough experience that losses and disappointments always open new gateways. And at some point all nests – whether meant to protect or confine us become too small to hold us any longer. Perhaps it is that as our soul expands we become, by nature, larger than that which currently holds us. And then – like a fledgling – we must venture up, out and away.

I stepped closer under the nest and spoke softly to the distraught, nest-bound bird. "You can do it, you know," I said gently. "Trust your instincts; try those wings!" And somewhere in the core of my heart I heard Someone great and bright and infinitely loving whispering those same encouragements to me – a bit eerie, I have to say, but also very real, and oh, so comforting.

Whether that little bird felt the same about the words I offered him will remain his secret. I do know that later that afternoon when I again checked the nest he was gone – out flying ecstatic circles around the barn, over the field across the road, back to the pine forest, down, down to the electric line between the house and barn to land beside his brothers and sisters. Then in a while they were rested up and once again with high-pitched chirps "my" wild, reckless swooping fledglings flung their little torpedo bodies joyfully through the air around me, testing and exploring the thermals and updrafts, fast-fluttering their wings while their anxious parents swept past me and around them in graceful, rocket-speed maneuvers.

For over a week now my little fledglings have explored their new world, returning to their nest in the barn each night – jostling their fat little bodies to try and fit the space, their watchful parents perched close by. At dawn, as dark sky turns to first deep blue, they once again leave nest and barn, chirping happily as they move outward into the new day. And so, at times I, too return to my nest – now built of memories of my two friends and inspirations for the days ahead as I look outward to better times.

When the air cools in a month or two my little birds will begin their grandest adventure of all – migrating south to winter-over in Central and South America. I will miss the little guys in the barn, their frantic cheeping when the parents brought insects, the little faces looking down inquisitively at me as twice daily I cleaned stalls and fed my animals. Empty Nest Syndrome, literally. But to see them flying! Testing their new freedom, leaving the confines of the high, rugged nest for the clean expanse of summer sky – all that I am is flying with them, rushing along the air currents in the broadness of sunlight. I am no longer sad and discouraged.

The little creatures careen through the boundless air, rest a while on the old dead pine tree, then push off again as if the sky's temptation is just too great. How much they remind me of the patterns and cycles of life – of everyone and everything around me. Did these birds leave behind their world of spirit to be born in a nest high up in my barn? Now they have left their nest behind them, to be born to a new world – for them – of endless sky and air and high tree limbs.

At winter's end they will leave their world in South America to once again travel north. Will they return to the world of my barn, to start families of their own in that nest of interwoven twigs carefully lined with soft donkey hair? And when it comes time for them to die from their physical existence, I would guess they will, once again, leave the "nest" of Earth. They will emerge from their swallow bodies to try their new, soul-form wings, and ride the thermals of the spirit world from where they once were born. What a grand adventure!

Hop Scotch and Leap Squirrel

WHEN I WAS A CHILD growing up in Connecticut I often played Hop Scotch on the sidewalk in front of my house. I rarely had others my age to play with and so I learned how to entertain myself, laying down a foundation for a lifelong determination to be strong and self-reliant. Hop Scotch filled so many early needs for me: drawing great, connected squares with colored chalks and then conquering those squares with a focused, forward motion, balance, and sweet success without having to depend on anyone. Always one who needed to find my own way no matter how hard I could – and did – fall flat on my face, early on in my Hop Scotch days I figured out how to make such a simple game more creative and challenging. I, master of my own success or failure, would draw more and more complicated, odd-shaped blocks, becoming quite adept at adding in imaginary tangled forests fraught with fiery dragons and giant, snarling bears – all to be avoided by landing just so on the correctly shaped and colored squares that would afford me safe passage through such a dangerous world. I always made it to safety, of course, making me quite the hero and bold adventurer.

When not forced by my well-meaning mother into ballet classes, piano practice, and having to behave myself "like a good little girl" I roamed happily in my true environment: nature. Trees, stones, bugs, turtles, squirrels, flowers and plants were my beloved companions; my blue two-wheeler bike was my horse, and I was the strong Native American warrior looking out for my tribe. Intuitively I knew everything had life – and as such, everything deserved to be treated with honesty and respect. Even the bears and dragons of my imagination, though to be avoided, were not enemies to me, just the shadows of those deep, hurting places within my all-too real human self. Nature was my collection of colored "squares", and I spent my young and pre-teen days maneuvering within them, ever forward, ever determined to make it safely one to the next.

When adolescence blind-sided me and I lost touch with which square to leap to next, those dragons and bears loomed over me and I wasn't always so successful in avoiding them. Still, there were the constants I had relied on as a child – the trees, the stones, the animals, wind and water – all those beings who never let me down, never criticized me for being who I innately was, who never had expectations of me that then turned to disappointment, desire to harm me, and eventual betrayal. My colored squares of safety and success were too often shrouded in murkiness until I found that one stone I could hold in my hand, or the song of a single bird, or the radiant open generosity of a flower – and then I was hopping forward, renewed, determined, that fierce warrior again.

As with most of our childhood games, Hop Scotch became long forgotten and those days of pretending to be a fierce, devoted warrior, protector of my tribe, dissolved into all the practical necessities of adult life. Those mythical dragons and bears, with new faces now, can still loom above me, yet I continue unquestioningly to find my best refuge and renewal in the natural world. But there are no squares of colored chalk on the sidewalk outside my back door.

Most recently, I became ill with a virus for which there seemed no solution except, as is the way with such things, time and patience. I had no desire for anything except to inch my way painfully through the days. Having once again fallen on my face, figuratively speaking of course, I was even too tired to try and be self-reliant, surrendering to whatever help the universe could offer me.

In the midst of my misery, I looked out the back door and down the Maple tree came a mother squirrel with two of her babies behind her. I could hear her chattering to them, as mothers will do, and could see her youngsters would have none of her scolding. She leapt to the high fence board that lines the dogs' garden, obviously heading to the roof of the house, then eventually to the bird feeders and trees in the front yard. Her children, as adventurous and creative as I had once been, bounded along behind her, one following the other. Then the one in back leapt right over the youngster in front, while that one, now in back, shuffled forward, leaping over his brother or sister in front of him – and so it went, a joyous version of Leap Frog, only more appropriately – Leap *Squirrel* to fit the occasion. The mother continued to scold right on up and over the roof, her rambunctious offspring leaping over each other in succession as they made their journey to the spruce tree on the other side. They made it just fine, and I, laughing, suddenly felt so much better. My tribe had returned after all and I was well on my way to yet another bright and balanced "square" in my life.

Given a box of colored chalks, I would have no doubt those young, head-strong squirrels would draw squares on my sidewalk and we could share a game of Hop Scotch. And maybe, if we were very brave, we would invite the dragons and bears to join us.

Jonathan Likes Me
Even if I am Not a Poodle

IN FACT, JONATHAN *ADORES* ME. I can't honestly say all the dogs I have shared space with have held such intense devotion, even though they knew me to be a dependable source of good food, clean water, cushy bedding, and unwavering loyalty.

Lisa comes first to mind. A small brown-and-white hound, she adopted me when, as a tiny pup, she burst yelping through our neighbors' boxwood hedge. She had announced herself next door first, but being immediately rejected, revamped her efforts and arrived full-tilt at our back door where the one-two *I'm Such an Adorable Puppy* sucker punch of course worked on us. She sized us up as useful to her, immediately took over the entire family and for the rest of her long life clearly only tolerated us as long as her basic needs were met. A dog's normally unswerving affection for his or her human family was as blatantly missing in Lisa's case as was respect for the basic rules of the house: No opening the refrigerator door and helping oneself to the contents. No breaking down the back door to get out whenever one feels like it. No standing over someone and barking in their face until said dog surrenders his/her cushion or human their place on the couch. She was the most self-absorbed dog I had, in my (then) forty years, ever met.

But not Jonathan, my all-black, curly-haired miniature heap of undying poodle devotion, love and affection. I am confident that in his doggy eyes I can do no wrong, even when I take him to the vet, am late with his dinner, or regretfully, step on his paw. Forgiveness is immediate and as long as I am in his line of sight, he is a happy fellow. Back when Rosie was alive, he had no reluctance sharing his bed with her (but then, she was his Significant Other), or a patch of sun with Calliope, the Jack Russell/beagle/whatever mix. If Lillie snarls at Jonathan when he wanders into her personal space, he simply turns around and walks in another direction. He knows and respects all the rules of the house, guards me against such intruders as crickets and stink bugs, and watches, patiently, my every move despite now being nearly blind with cataracts in both eyes. He is my personal fan club. And, I am his.

When, at the age of 15, Lisa crossed that famous Rainbow Bridge, we did miss that brazen, selfish, no-rules little hound, but have to admit that the household of humans, cats and dogs breathed a sigh of relief. Tape was removed from the refrigerator door, and no one feared the loss of their bed. We think of her with fondness, a good laugh, and a shake of our heads.

But – also – when *I* think about Lisa I see a side of myself that can be dismayingly similar: self-absorbed, demanding, closed-minded to the basic rules of respect for others. While I would like to think that I am completely generous, envy, self-pity, and desire can slip in and distract me from being the person that I really want to be all the time: " She has a bigger piece of chocolate cake than I do;" "Everyone else gets time off, why can't I?" "When is it going to be *my* turn?" That sort of thing. And that kind of small and petty attitude, what I might call my Lisa-Self, isn't much fun to be around, from my own perspective or anyone else who has to endure it. So I actually can thank Lisa for showing me exactly the way I *don't* want to behave.

But when I remember to become my Jonathan-Self, everyone likes my company, just the way I, equally, love to be in Jonathan's company. A mutual-admiration, utterly devoted, let-me-tag-along-beside-you kind of relationship. If I remember to just walk away from another's angry or disrespectful onslaught; if I can have so much room in my heart that I can share that space with all manner of people; and if I can, like Jonathan, look past another person's moodiness and see only their innate loveliness and like them just for who they are, not because they have to be like me, or agree with me; if, like Jonathan, I behave in all the appropriate ways, then I find I like myself much better as well.

Of course, for Jonathan, and the majority of dogs (by their very nature) focused love and loyalty is instinctive – they don't have to stop and evaluate how their doing. But I get off track easily. Fortunately for me, my little poodle shows me with beautiful constancy that he still adores me, even if I am, at times, way too human and forget to be my Jonathan-Self. Now pushing the venerable age of 18, he continues to bounce along like a puppy, be enthralled with every meal and treat, and love me, as the saying goes, to the moon and back. He is, without question, my hero.

Redefining Perfection, Calliope-Style

So it seems an appropriate time to talk about Calliope because while she, somewhat like Lisa, tended towards independence and just a bit of self-absorption, she was always sweet and affectionate and tailored her own desires to those of the team, being our family of humans and critters. While always knowing exactly what she wanted, she was willing to bend if necessary, a trait Lisa never could claim.

Calliope was three months old when we met, homeless and desperately in pain from both hips being completely fractured. But she had courage and determination and youth on her side, how could she not survive? A fascinating mix of Beagle, Jack Russell, and Dachshund, this little tan-and-white jewel was the master of cleverness artfully spiked by enthusiasm. Nothing daunted her. She was the supreme artist of her own true self and totally fine with it.

Calliope defined her daily schedule by the availability of food and "treats" – put into quotes because she and I had different concepts of what constitutes a treat and when it should be available to her. Considering she had weight issues most of her long life, an insatiable hunger, and no scruples whatsoever, we were often at odds – no, downright war – over what and when "treats" were appropriate.

For Calliope, anytime was a good time, quite acceptable in her eyes. As for content? Pulling down the basket that blocks the stairs to access Emma's bowl of dry cat food was good, better than all other treats combined. Something about those little stars of chicken and brown rice. Her enthusiasm unleashed as it was at such times, she often would inadvertently push the cat bowl off the stairs with her nose, sending cascades of kibble down to the anxious and grateful mouths of Jonathan and Rosie. Calliope had yet to master tempering her enthusiasm with caution that she might retain all rights (and little food stars) for herself.

Second on her list of favorites was Emma's litter box, safely positioned behind a pair of gates intended to keep roaming dogs away from it. Hardly. In her canine wisdom, assisted by toenails that had brain cells imbedded in them, Calliope learned how to work the gates apart *just so* with a rocking motion that eventually separated the latch bolt at the top, laying vulnerable the feast before her.

Further down on her list was the trash bin under the sink. Jarring the cabinet doors open with her shoulder, while effective, could prove time-consuming, attention-(mine)-drawing, and ultimately far more work than either the cat bowl or box, for there was usually less that was tasty contained therein, careful as I am with recycling and waste.

This lovely albeit challenging creature, would temporarily suspend her food search to snuggle down on the sofa, a pillow tucked under her head, another behind her back, and a third by her tail. Her talent at pillow-adjustment was inspiring; perhaps two minutes would consume her efforts to arrange and rearrange her comfort zone. She slept deeply, completely unaffected by the fact that not ten minutes ago we had probably had a "discussion" over her insistence that with a bit of help from her super-intelligent toes, the refrigerator door would open revealing a bounty that would stagger even her expectations. Did she cower beneath my raised voice? Did she feel remorse for disturbing my rare moment of peace? Barely – just a hint to let me know she really had *meant* to observe the rules.

In her eyes, she, and her world were perfect. Everything she undertook, even *considered* undertaking – well-thought out or improvised – was perfect, was exactly as it should be, according, that is, to Calliope. She had no regrets, no sense of failure. Should her efforts at stealing cat food be thwarted, no problem – more opportunities were bound to arise the next time Emma asked for her bowl to be placed on the stairs. There would always be new trash under the sink, and as for the litter box – food in Emma's bowl seemed to naturally, if not magically, lead to treats in the box. And Calliope knew how to work patience.

And so Calliope's philosophy of life appeared to be: What is emptied, refills; what is consumed must, according to the laws of nature, re-materialize in new form, be it trash or poops in the litter box. Above all, unquestionable faith in such a giving universe combined with ingenuity and persistence certainly pays off. Accordingly, becoming stressed over the availability of what one needs or desires is senseless; and when in between treat opportunities: arrange one's pillows on the sofa knowing that a decent rest simply fills the time in a sensible fashion until the universe once again provides.

That, it would seem, is perfection, Calliope-style. She would probably suggest this chapter be called *Going with the Flow: From Cat Bowl to Litter Box to Calliope;* or *From Fridge to Table to Trash Bin to Calliope.* Notice that all roads seemed to lead to a very clever little creature of enormous faith in the workings of a generous and timely universe. But while I speak often of the perfect workings of nature and the universe, all *my* roads seem to lead to doubt, confusion, and fear. Fear of not having enough; fear of failing at my chosen craft; fear of falling victim to yes, what I am told (and believe) by the media or others, that we live in an imperfect, dysfunctional social, economic, environmental and political system called, oddly enough, Modern Civilization.

I do know, deep in my soul's connection to All That Is, that in truth nothing/no one could possibly exist as we do if there was not an underlying perfection to it all. Even to whatever appears to be chaotic and distorted, lacking or impaired. I have yet to fully mentally grasp the how and why of that perfection, it's just a knowing that keeps coming back to me.

Much as it seemed to be with my sweet, determined hound mix who, when not in active mode, would lie deeply asleep, toes twitching as she most likely dreamed of cat kibble cascading down around her. And from experience – hers and mine – would such a possibility transform into probability and later into reality as her thoughts delved into the deliciousness involved.

Calliope had no doubts about the perfection of her world; why should I about mine?

Fiesta

BEING GARDENERS WITH LARGE ANIMALS, each year we designate a new place for piles of critter manure. With three piles in rotation, each spring we have well-seasoned compost for the various vegetable and flower gardens. All manner of interesting "volunteers" sprout in the compost from daffodils to watermelon. One June I noticed the first leaves of what appeared to be a squash plant on the newest compost pile. From a few broad leaves quickly sprang a green vine with tiny feelers that reached out tentatively across the mounded soil.

I didn't figure it had much of a chance. If the donkeys didn't eat it, they would probably trample it. The summer looked to be a dry one, but I had enough to water in the other gardens, and decided to let it find its own way to the nutrients it needed. Surely it had a plan? I figure everything has a plan built into it someplace, even on a subconscious level, certainly on a superconscious, or quantum soup level that physicists talk about. After all, without a plan, be it genetic code, intuition, instinct, or consciously constructed an acorn would try to grow into a monkey, and a monkey would think it should be part of the water cycle. You can see how chaos and confusion would reign. To keep it short, nothing would work as it was designed to, nor be what it needs to be.

So obviously, the squash had a plan.

I've worked with animals enough to realize that sometimes one's plan involves a short life – pop in, so-to-speak, have a good look around, then head back to the other side of here. To those of us who anticipate a long and joyful relationship, that plan seems cruel and unfair. Where was a chance at life? Why so young? What went wrong? From experience, the conclusion I have come to is that age has nothing to do with living, and nothing goes "wrong". Even a moment of being on this dimension is worth the trip, and sometimes, it is all that is needed – this time around. Maybe next time, that soul will be a sea turtle and live hundreds of years. Who knows for sure, only time and again there seems to be a logical reason for everything and everyone that/who happens. Some stories are brief sentences; others are epic novels a thousand pages long... same with life. I have read those thousand-page novels and some are too long and very boring whereas some of those one-sentence stories are powerful and memorable.

Back to the squash.

Each morning when I dumped the wheelbarrow of its manure load on the currently-seasoning pile, I would check on what now had become of my squash. She had developed several more vines going in six directions, wider leaves, and the most astonishingly beautiful large, orange-golden flowers. One of the blossoms had developed a small squash at its base.

One morning I noticed most of the leaves had been eaten by deer who visit our little woods at night. I wasn't particularly sad; it seemed appropriate enough to me that a wild little plant should be consumed by a wild creature who would eventually pass its manure on to the forest floor, fertilizer for new plants. And, I had not yet named my squash so the attachment was not as strong. I congratulated myself for my ability to stand down and allow.

But the squash plant seemed to be re-invigorated by the deers' pruning and before long new vines and new leaves began sprouting, as if on a Very Determined Path, a plan not to be terminated. The donkeys did trampled it, July and August brought a scarcity of rain, and the remaining leaves looked dry and riddled with holes from some insect who fancies squash leaves.

I had a lot on my plate then, as did most of the country, Europe, and Asia. A crumbling economy, a recently retired husband suffering from depression, my own aches and pains, and 100 degree days left me little energy for the squash plant other than a quick greeting each morning. Somehow I sensed it was wild, would survive or not, and apparently strong of character was fine with the way its life was playing out. So, I let it be. If only it could be that easy with everyone in my life.

Somewhere in that summer the East Coast, including this property, experienced a rare earthquake that had everyone talking. Then it was Irene, a hurricane of enormous proportions, barreling up the East Coast, one of the worst storms in history. The Stock Market plummeted again and along with it, much of the retirement savings I have to live on the rest of my life. I found it hard to be very positive in my attitude as I pushed a full and heavy wheelbarrow out to the poop pile each day.

I did check on the one squash – now clearly a fiesta squash, round and cheerful in its colorful stripes – that not only had survived trampling donkey feet, nibbling deer, and drought, but had continued to ripen nicely. I had, over the past few weeks, pondered whether I should eventually harvest it, or since it appeared to be the only squash on the now once again expanding vines, to go back to ground. I wondered what the squash, itself, would choose?

As I rounded the long red gate separating the donkeys' middle field from the woods, I looked up into one of the most spectacular creations I have seen. The plant, started from a single, errant seed, had not only survived catastrophic circumstances, but gone on to spread in a most unusual manner. Now vines were everywhere – pouring through the bars of the gate, up into and around densely growing, six-foot stalks of pokeweed, many of them already laden with the deep red berries that feed the birds over winter. Two more ripening squashes perched between branches high above the ground, one braced against the fence line the gate is attached to, the other a good four feet up. More were starting at the bases of large, orange and golden blossoms now glowing with light, everywhere amongst the poke berries.

All on her own – from birth to fruition – my squash plant had executed her plan to survive, *to thrive*, and to demonstrate how to keep striding forward through apparent adversity and keep climbing, keep blooming, keep giving back. I was impressed by such determination; impressed enough to have a look around at my own plan and put a bit more effort into knowing who I am, why I am here, and what I am going to do next.

I now know that absolutely the squash in question had a plan, and that plan was to be the best squash it could be – not a monkey, certainly not an oak tree, and definitely not a quitter. Irene, the now infamous hurricane, pounded wind and rain at my house and barn, but if the squash vine could hang on for the ride, I knew I could hang on for whatever ride life handed me. It's all worth blossoming over.

I finally decided to not name my squash, realizing that in truth, she was her own squash, doing a spectacular job being just that, the squash she was born to be. I could no longer claim her as mine – she was a squash of the ground, the forest, the air and the water that nourish her. She was a squash of the deer and insects as their food. I reckon she could be considered a universal, quantum field squash. But most especially, I believe she was a squash of hope, joy, and radiant beauty, rightly named, Fiesta.

Insight with Soapy Water

I SAW IT AS A small miracle – probably a bigger one for me than for the creature in question, a ladybug who had tumbled into my soapy dishwater. Gone – they always are, delicate beings – they drown so quickly. I scooped it out with my finger and, *What?* One leg wobbled, then another, then another – my dismay ceased and now ecstatic, I carried the wee one to a sunny windowsill in my little garden room where it walked with perfect balance on firm ground to the nearest plant. I returned to my task of washing the morning dishes, singing as I cleaned, for in my opinion, I had just participated in an event worthy of celebration.

Since early childhood I have been "rescuing" things – first there were bugs and frogs, followed by a rabbit I named Sneakers, and when I hit adulthood I was full stride into dogs, cats, chickens, (yes, a couple of roosters in distress as well), goats, wild birds, ducks, more bugs, more frogs, and of course, the crowning glory, my beloved bovine companion Christina. All of it has been a lovely adventure and a lot of hard work on many levels for decades and I have not one regret. But I do have new thoughts on the whole process called "rescue."

If I were to be really truthful here, I would have to admit that while I was busy embracing various species in need, each and every one of them in one way or another, was just as busy embracing – rescuing if you will – me. Team effort, the wounded supporting one another, two or four footed, webbed, hoofed, clawed, finned – rescuer and rescued as one unit, we have always leaned on one another, lifted one another out of the soapy dishwater of daily life with all its conflicts and trials, and across all interspecies communication barriers have we pledged our shared Heart to one another.

Delving deeper into speculation here, I also wonder who or what, then, lifts *us* out of the dilemmas we find ourselves in, and carries us to higher, firmer ground? I ask such questions on a daily basis because from personal, unshakable experience, I can attest to the fact that we are not alone in the struggles we so often find ourselves swimming around in. I promise you: there is, absolutely, unseen help looking out for us, that gentle, concerned "finger" to lift us to a better position where we can shake the soapy watery parts of life off of ourselves and find stability beneath our proverbial feet once again.

My little ladybug had no concept of what actually happened in those frantic few seconds of her near-death experience. She fell quite by accident into something frothy and way too wet, the world as she knew it giving her no support with which to save herself. But suddenly she was airlifted by the grace of something mysterious and placed with care onto solid ground. And off she strode, life continuing – at least for then – with no answers even if she had questions as to what and who had saved her.

As with just about everything in the natural world (and recalling Mo and the field mouse), I believe had she perished beneath the soapy water she would have simply moved out of her no-longer functioning physical body and moved on in another plane of existence. While I delighted in keeping her from death, perhaps death would have been just as fine with her. Now, the process of that transition from one state of being to another can certainly be frightening and painful, but after that – well, only the ladybug could really say how she would have viewed it. What does seem apparent to me after all these years of saving and rescuing and, likewise, shepherding creatures over the Rainbow Bridge, is that what I have really done is to lift someone struggling on their own and in need of immediate assistance, to a place and position of peace, thereby releasing the bonds of fear, pain, and or despair to help that lovely one walk forward – in renewed life, or renewed spirit, all one and the same.

I will always save anyone in distress; I will rush around and call for professional help and stay up long, endless nights to ease the suffering of another. "Bless me into usefulness..." is the daily prayer in the Buddhist practice of compassion and lovingkindness. I'm not entirely sure this is rescuing though, more just being Who I Am – and who so many – humans *and* creatures *and* unseen, Angelic assistants – are as well: leaving the heart's door wide open and the welcome mat out, knowing we are all in this adventure of life together with all its soapy water but also its firm and sunny windowsills.

Field Flowers

"WEEDS ARE FLOWERS TOO, ONCE you get to know them," said Eeyore, in *Winnie-The-Pooh*, by A.A. Milne. What a perfect tenet to live by... this could be also translated as, There are no weeds, only flowers, and how applicable this becomes to everything in our lives.

Plants typically considered to be weeds in gardens and manicured lawns, my mother, who respected all life, referred to as field flowers, wild and free to grow as they pleased rather than selected and planted by human beings. This appealed to her, a woman who had, since early childhood, wanted to be a gypsy. Damaged by her father, and then her husband (my father), her spirit so often struggled to toss off the burdens of shame, sorrow, anger and pain. To her, a dandelion daring to pop up in the middle of her lawn was a lovely demonstration of courage and strength. She always allowed the dandelions to remain, much to the disgust and chagrin of her small-community neighbors. But, like the dandelions, she was not afraid to stand tall, toss back her head, and shine.

When she was in her late sixties she moved from Massachusetts to Virginia to a small town ten miles from me and bought a ranch house in a subdivision where manicured lawns were expected.

My mother, however, had other ideas. Over the years she lived in Orchard Acres, her lawn slowly transformed from neatly mowed grass to a small forest, full of young cedar trees, all manner of wild flowers, blackberry brambles and winding paths. Needless-to-say, she was the talk of the neighborhood.

Rather than be embarrassed by my mother's desire for wild nature, I admired her for it and find the same impulse flowing through my veins. The gypsy spirit lives on.

This spring, I planted two kinds of seeds in the whiskey barrel planter in the Dogs' Garden: miniature zinnias in the center with miniature sunflowers in a circle around them. Something about putting seeds into soil and the breathless, anxious waiting out the two weeks or so for signs of life, you just can't beat it. And I was not disappointed – gentle watering and good strong sun hoisted tiny sprouts to the surface, until within a week it seemed all the seeds were now tiny plants, and all looked the same. Nevertheless, I was undaunted and decided to see just what ended up where.

As the seedlings continued to develop, all still looking oddly similar in leaf structure, one in particular caught my attention. "That's *not* a sunflower," my gardener son, Michael proclaimed, peering over the new flower crop. I pointed out that the leaves were similar enough we should let it be. However, as the plants grew, then buds formed it became increasingly evident that we had a volunteer stranger in the whiskey barrel. Not a miniature zinnia; not a miniature sunflower; still – it had courage and presence.

And so, I have assured it, it may stay – not a weed or intruder, but a field flower, now part of our family and quite obviously a fellow gypsy.

Namaste

WHILE SITTING ON THE FLOOR with Jonathan, I noticed the tiniest of ants carrying a rather large bread crumb in her mouth as she moved with determination across the floor. My first thought was not:

OH my god I have ants! Nor was it:

Yuck! Or:

Hmmm, best to get rid of it right now, I hope there aren't more...

No, my initial reaction was curiosity, admiration for her efforts, and kinship. For you see what I also saw was the mental image of myself happily clutching a package as I walked up from the mailbox by the road. For I would know that package contained a new book or other treasure. And I had just as much determination and joyful anticipation as that tiny ant with her bread crumb. How many times had I carried a friend's letter or package up the drive; how many times had my little ant friend carried a morsel of food across the floor? Did that make us soulmates?

Of course, my brain got to work as it so often does regarding the "others" of the natural world. I thought on the birds now singing so beautifully for the nestlings they are raising and how protective they are of their offspring. I, too, would sing joyously about my two sons, Michael and Tim, if I had the opportunity, but nonetheless, my love overflows. And I would do anything to keep them safe.

Snowy, my devoted dog who follows me everywhere and sleeps by my shoulder at night, tirelessly pads behind me when I go outside, or climb the stairs to my office, or move from living room to kitchen to front porch. She follows, sits or lies down, gets up, follows... and I can almost hear her say to me,

Rita, sit – stay, please! (sigh)

Just the other day I said to her as she turned circles on the couch, making her comfy "nest", *Snowy, please! Settle down! (sigh)*.

There are endless connections between us all, be it human to creature to wind to stone to tree to mountain to river... we are strong and rooted, but also can bend with the fluctuations of events. We suffer and rejoice, are young, age, grow old, move on. (Yes, mountains are "born" and "die", too). We all share so much, and if we look closely enough, "me" and "not me" become simply, "us" – a beautiful, interwoven garment of mutual existence.

"Namaste." It's an ancient Sanskrit greeting meaning *I bow to you,* an acknowledgment that there is a spark of Divinity within all beings that is located within the heart, and when I meet another being, human, creature, tree, etc., I offer my respect. And so to my little ant, I bowed and whispered *Namaste.* The ant scurried on, I thought on the book that would be soon arriving in my mailbox, and Jonathan ate his breakfast. All was as it should be.

In all honesty, there are times I become annoyed when what or who I expect to show up in my life does not, or when my day starts by everything going wrong and I fuss and mope and feel the victim. It was, in fact, that way today until I stepped outside into the morning air and took a deep breath. All around me everything was breathing, just as I was, but so easily and non-stressed: the plants, the trees, the bees gathering pollen, and I could almost feel the whole planet breathing in and breathing out in perfect rhythm.

I looked down at my feet to a patch of gravel and rocks. Directly in the center was a small, vibrant plant with tiny green leaves and yellow star-like blossoms. It looked so friendly and optimistic, as if calling to me: "Hey! Down here! Don't you see? If I can not only exist, but *thrive* in the midst of this rocky soil, so can you." And I knew the rest of my day would be just fine, and it has been. I just had to change how I looked at it all.

And so to the tiny ant, the determined plant, to the entire cosmos and all the world – *Namaste.*

Promise

I'M WRITING THIS ON A very stormy Saturday in mid-November. Rain drives sideways in great waves across the 40-acre field on the other side of the road from here and wind pummels the last of remaining leaves from deciduous trees. The sky, wrapping fog around me, lightens, then turns the sky dark and ominous in a second, as if the turbulent atmosphere itself would crash down to meet the Earth.

A cold front approaches: strong enough to drive near 70 degree temperatures to the 40s overnight and turn lingering rain showers to light snow. Everywhere people grumble about the weather, wishing it were spring arriving, not winter.

Earlier this morning, I slogged through water over my boots as I cleaned stalls and fed the donkeys. My head bent down inside my raincoat hood, I pushed a manure-filled wheelbarrow through thick mud and stacked clean hay into dry corners of the barn. I thought about how much the weather reminded me of the times we are all experiencing – wild and unpredictable, often dark, unsettling and downright frightening. How "stuck" we see ourselves, pushing through stalled lives and gloomy economic forecasts. So what's to celebrate in this rising holiday season?

Large animal chores done for the morning, I closed the feed shed door and stepped away from the barn. Wind was building in the mountains – like a boulder gathering speed as it rolls downhill, the roaring mounted as trees bent before it. I looked up at the sound and my raincoat fell away from my face. Just above me the clouds were forming layer upon layer, those closest to me flying from west to east. Each of many layers above the first seemed to move more slowly until suddenly a hole emerged. Through all the darkness, all the movement, all the wind and rain and fog: one hole straight up and up and up to a parting layer of white cloud completely stationary, blazing with sunlight.

And still on up through the parted clouds past the shimmering white – and there it was, cobalt- blue sky: the epitome of serenity, what is always there behind even the most ferocious of storms.

There was a break in the rain now but had it been a deluge I doubt I would have noticed. I could only stand in silence and awe, staring up through that gap in the swirling trails of cloud and fog, through and up to the clear pool blue of unfettered sky.

That's it, I thought, *what I need to reach for, to remember that beyond all the breakdown of what I thought was safe and secure lies that one "place" of undisturbed peace I can absolutely count on to always be there.*

As I walked on back to the house I stopped to look up at the old Maple tree as her brown, curled leaves fell steadily to the ground around me. With the leaves gone, how much more light came through the branches and into the kitchen window. Some people say the trees look dead in winter. Not at all in my opinion – they are sleeping now, gathering strength for that first push of spring. Reaching up to one of the lower branches I touched a newly-formed, tightly closed bud that had emerged from the place where a leaf had recently let go.

How appropriate; could I do the same? Could I, too, find the fresh start amid the releasing of the old ways? Something, it would seem, we are all being called to do these days.

I might call it 'Promise.' Not an ending, not even a beginning, certainly not hope, which implies 'maybe it might happen.' No, Nature the great teacher says *Here is my promise: behind the clouds no matter how thick, is endless clear sky; behind the falling, aged leaf is renewed life; and that very same falling away only lets in more light.*

While sitting here at my desk writing out my thoughts, a ladybug appeared on the inside windowsill and began moving along with purpose toward the screen. I knew he (or she) was searching for a way outside, and, always glad to help a fellow traveler I scooped the little creature onto a piece of paper and carried him (or her) downstairs and out the door. Despite a light rain falling, the tiny being climbed up along my outstretched hand until, reaching the tip of my finger, the ladybug spread minute wings and lifted skyward, rising higher and higher into the branches of the Maple. At that moment nothing could have been more beautiful to me.

Tiny Adventures

LAST YEAR, THE DISTANCE FOCUSING mechanism on my Canon camera failed, leaving pictures fuzzy and useless. While really upsetting to me at first, I discovered what did continue to work perfectly was the macro, or close-up setting. Curious, I began exploring deep inside of flowers, a single drop of dew along a grass stem, one tiny bug, heart-shaped bits of watermelon, even the intricate pattern of an ice crystal in winter.

What at first I had grumbled over as a limitation in my equipment became instead a door opening to a whole new world, one I had often overlooked in my quest for the "bigger picture." Now, rather than standing back for a wide-angle view of the whole garden for example, I moved my lens into the heart of a single leaf or blossom, to find miraculous colors, designs, light and even visiting creatures I never would have otherwise seen, a miniature universe unto its self.

Sometimes it does seem as if it is the tiniest of things that can lead us back to the Whole.

Grounding Stone

THE SCRAGGLY YOUNG VIRGINIA PINE clung tenaciously to the outcropping of rock high up in the Blue Ridge Mountains, its roots winding deep into tiny crevices and anchoring it, by some miracle, to the concrete-like clay soil below. Wind whipped the small brave soul but I heard no complaints, only the soft sound of pine needles bending and curving into the cool autumn gusts.

The Blue Ridge, the ancient, gentle range that holds my home and heart, is Sanctuary for me — ever a source of inspiration, strength and awe. Consider that some of the granite found in these particular mountains is over one *billion* years old, formed even before there was life on Earth. What history these mountains have seen! How much they have to tell us if we were attuned enough to hear their voice.

I sat down next to the little pine and wondered: Had there been, some many years ago, conversation between the tree's seedling as it floated on the wind, and the rock face?

"Rest here; I'll give you ground to hold you firm as you grow, even in the strongest gales," the mountain would have offered. I would imagine the seedling was glad to finally take root in such an inviting friend. Perhaps, as Indigenous Peoples believe (and so do I), the mountains themselves are conscious Beings with spirit,

heart, and love. Then of course they would invite the trees and grasses, bear and deer, rabbits and birds and all manner of insects and bugs – the infinite scope of species to keep them company through the years, decades, centuries, and ages.

I recently saw a TV program that stated unequivocally that scientists have now discovered that the ocean as a whole is a sentient being, much the way the planet – Gaia – is a living, breathing entity in "her" own right, even has her own sound, a song now able to be heard on the most sophisticated of equipment. This all gives one much to think about and a great deal of reconsideration to be done, unless one already knows, or at least senses this.

Sitting on that slab of granite with my knees tucked up under my chin against the wind, it was not difficult to feel as if rock and I shared the same breath and the little tree, all the trees filling the mountain range, clouds and creatures, wind and sun, all breathing in and breathing out, a collective expression of life in its most expansive, unbounded definition. Life just flowed so easily between everything, in wavelike motion as that of the sea and the light traversing through the atmosphere. I felt as if I were sitting amongst old and very dear friends. I would have to leave the mountain ridges soon, obligations called me back down to my own little piece of the Blue Ridge, but I would return. How could I not?

The Dance of Bugs and Birds

THEY WERE EVERYWHERE IN THE afternoon sunlight, an infinite number of tiny winged creatures moving at enormous speeds in no particular pattern. When I looked at the air where there was no sunlight, I saw no insects, but I knew they were there and the whirling, dancing patterns they drew would stretch endlessly beyond just outside the barn where I presently stood, to the lawn, the road, the field beyond...perhaps even up into the mountains rimming the horizon.

I had watched them over the years from this same doorway leading from the barn to the field, always admiring them but not knowing why, except that they are life, worthy of respect and appreciation. This time I knew something different – seeing them perhaps with new vision, a new understanding I had not had before. Of the thousands filling the air before me, with an impeccable sense of accuracy no one was crashing into, let alone merely bumping into, anyone else. What did each sense about those around them that kept them at precise and safe distances, simultaneously creating a fluidity and continuity to the overall collective? Mesmerized, I stood out of time, watching them in case I was wrong and one – even just that one, would collide with its neighbor.

But it didn't happen.

A day later I was in town; the roads were full of vehicles, horns honking, people shouting out car windows, some cutting others off in traffic, some trying to change lanes without success because no one wanted to let them in… we've all been there. It's what we dread. Sirens were audible in three directions; I passed two fender-benders and saw a third barely avoided. Giant SUVs barreled past compacts and minis, obscuring everyone's line of vision.

At a stoplight I looked up and above me was a flock of birds of maybe thirty or more, moving as one unit: swooping down, turning, flapping together then drifting, all as if there was a conductor or dance master directing them… "Two, three, four everyone turn…" How do they know? Why don't they collide with one another? What silent knowing or sensing keeps them in such perfect and harmonious movement? I've watched such flocks many times and always I am awed by them.

What do the insects and birds have that we do not? I would guess they have no ego, for one. And not having ego to blind and deafen them, they move to the rhythm of the Universal Energy Field, that which connects one and all to the One and the All.

For the most part, we humans rely on intellect to draw up the laws, rules, divisions and levels that help us to co-exist in a somewhat non-chaotic manner. But we do bump into one another in so many ways, usually blaming the other for our colliding. Accidental or intentional it's all the same. Have we lost that instinct, that intuitive sense the creatures have? Bruised, busted, broken, lame, too often we limp away from our encounters with one another, with other beings, and often with ourselves and dread the inevitability of going out again into a seemingly unsafe world.

Where, for us, is the choreographed dance that comes so naturally to countless creatures, that sense of perfect relationship to all the others moving with them in this third-dimensional world? Can we, as a species, leave our egos behind once and for all and move respectfully among the animals, birds, reptiles, insects and all aspects of our planet? How wonderful to never dread our encounters with anyone again, to live in a current of harmony that has no boundaries, where the only "bumping into" becomes instead, an embracing. Can we as human beings do the same one day? I know we can.

Perspective

Running to my car, face down against a bitter winter wind, I wondered when spring was ever going to arrive in Virginia. *Not soon enough*, I thought, as a rubbed my gloved hands together to try and keep them warm. Later that afternoon I broke ice in water buckets, shoveled frozen manure from the donkeys' room in the barn, and fussed as I raced against the quickly fading daylight. *Not my favorite time of year*, I muttered between chattering teeth.

That night it snowed. On schedule my three old dogs, Snowy, Jonathan, and Lillie had to make their last run to the outside "facilities." I opened the back door to the eerie surprise of snow, already a good two inches deep, sparkling in the floodlights as it thickly swirled and blew around us.

Lillie, little bit of a dog that she is, was not pleased and backed rapidly around my feet to the warm dryness of the kitchen behind us. Snowy ploughed forth, her thick white coat perfect for such events, and immediately began happily shoveling the powdery stuff with her eager nose. Ancient Jonathan chose to attend to business without delay, winced his eyes against the chilly crystals, and goal accomplished, tracked a swift retreat to the back door.

I should have called Snowy in and returned to bed. I did

have a full day ahead of me and now it looked as if shoveling snow might be a large part of it. But I was as entranced as Snowy, both of us standing there in the silent streaming snow, our noses turned upward with delight. I wasn't even cold.

Back inside, my furry three curled back into their beds and slept. I couldn't. For almost an hour I sat by the window and watched the snow, felt such a deep intimacy with the flakes as they danced by me to add their sparkling selves to the ever growing accumulation on trees and ground, and fence lines and barn. Finally, I went back to bed and dreamt of making snow forts for snowball fights and building snowmen and dogs, even a snow cat.

By daylight the snow had stopped. It was a perfect snow – not so deep it had to be shoveled for hours, but enough to transform the entire environment into a new and enticing adventure.

The sun broke the mountains' edge, sent waves of color flying like joyous sledders down the smooth and sloping hills across the road. Trees, as if frosted with thick whipped cream, gleamed and shimmered. Brilliantly red male cardinals crowded around the bird feeders with blue jays and squirrels. Mourning doves paired up with other ground feeders – tiny English sparrows and juncos. Fast darting gold finches teamed with purple finches and a lone Indigo bunting, tapping at the thistle seed feeder. And in the barn my donkeys gratefully chewed piles of fresh hay.

Snowy and I took our morning walk through our two acre forest, while flickers and woodpeckers hammered on dead trees above us. Two white-tailed deer who had been resting by the back fence, rose and stood to watch us pass not ten yards away. Rabbit, raccoon and opossum tracks zig-zagged across the path, around trees, under fallen pines and out again.

And everywhere the air smelled so clean.

Later that evening, after the sun had set and the day's final barn work was done, I stood under emerging stars. Soft moonlight settled across the forest and the fields, and last birds tucked in for the night leaving a small dusting of music echoing through the foothills. Cold; crystalline; crunchy under my feet. I couldn't get enough of it – yes, winter.

Ice and sleet storms are no fun at all, until the sun returns and sets everything ablaze. Impassible country roads such as I live on are challenging, especially when one of the animals has a medical emergency. And hurrying back from town to get outside chores done before dark – truly frustrating.

But longer hours of darkness mean more time by the fire with a cup of hot chocolate and a favorite book. Stars come out earlier and stay longer and there is a subtle sense of peace from slumbering trees.

Standing on my hill under the stars, my breath swirling around me, I decided to not hurry winter away, nor wish for an early spring. What is now, is perfect, is just the way it should be….and at this precise moment, it is my favorite time of year.

Simarouba
(and more about Paradise)

I SUPPOSE THIS MUST BE paradise, this lovely plot of land on which I live and thrive. Surrounded by the Blue Ridge Mountains, companioned by animals, birds and insects of various species both wild and domestic and enchanted by plants and trees of every imaginable kind, how appropriate that a small seedling should suddenly appear dead center on the front rock wall. Any seedling? Hardly, for this one is *Simarouba glauca,* otherwise known as the Paradise tree.

The tree began its upward journey last fall as a volunteer, most like dropped in infant pod-stage by a passing bird. How thoughtful, for while it rested/slept throughout the cold winter months, by early spring it was ascending skyward by the moment. And now, in late August it stands as high as the house- easily 30 feet, with a spread of boughs that is cool and impressive.

Simarouba glauca (pronounced in a rolling sound: Sim-uh-ROO-buh CLAW-kuh) easily grows to 40 feet and with such enthusiasm, I believe for it might be possible to sit with a cup of coffee and in an hour actually watch it grow. And enthusiasm is not a misplaced description, for Paradise trees are springing up all over the place.

Still, *Simarouba* has its critics. One person denigrated this tropical beauty as a "trash tree" – whatever that means, it cannot be positive. In fact, *Simarouba* is of the canopy-forming species, usually found in Florida and south. Perhaps it is global warming that brings it to Virginia.

Whatever the miracle that lands one of my favorite trees here at my small sanctuary for everything that lives, it is a miracle I share with birds and squirrels, even a raccoon or two balancing along the gracefully bending limbs that reach out and up. Out in back of the barn a young doe – one of many deer, often stands beneath one of the older, more mature Paradise trees, nibbling at shoots of grass and poke weed. Now, three new trees have started in the front pasture that belongs to the donkeys, and with *Simarouba's* habit of rapid growth, already the donkeys have shade under which to stand on a hot and humid day.

I really don't "suppose" that this must be paradise; I already *know* it is, always did from the moment my family and I chose this house and property as our home – 39 years ago. We have no plans to move. Could any place be as beautiful? Vibrant by day, still and magical by night – when often the only sound is an owl close by, or packs of coyotes calling back and forth across the mountains. In spring come the peepers in ponds and streams and summer there are Whip-poor-wills at dusk and dawn, gatekeepers of the close and opening of day.

Thinking on the concept of paradise, I find it everywhere – even in the bleakness that can roar up on anyone. Paradise can be a Morning Glory blossom; certainly paradise is found in cloud formations: the long, wispy wing-like ones or the tall white-topped clouds, tipped gold by the setting sun.

Paradise is in the call of the Carolina wren, or the White-throat sparrow. Paradise is watching two young squirrels playing chase up and down the maple tree – awe and laughter and joy that arises just opening my eyes and ears to all that is around me.

I look down and a tiny beetle scurries across a grass blade. Sunlight glistens off the opulent beetle's shell, a pinprick of glory against vibrant green. Looking up there are the mountains, robin egg's blue in the summer haze, gentle and rounded from eons of weathering. I would not have to even wonder at their intelligence – strong and wise, they speak of stamina and endurance.

Paradise is where we find it, if we choose to, if we really feel it's worth the journey. And the journey is not necessarily going someplace, just being still and in wonderment, opening to what is all around us.

Today, I have one favorite: *Simarouba glauca* – Paradise that found a place on our front rock wall and took root in my heart.

Ode to a Stink Bug
(my friend the "pest")

THE LITTLE STINK BUG WALKED purposefully along the windowsill toward the glass doors, but as I approached it stopped and turned, looking up at me. It didn't show fear, but curiosity, or simply acknowledgement of my presence. I meant no harm; perhaps it understood. Carefully, I lifted it into my hand and carried it outside into the air. Sensing freedom, it walked to the end of my outstretched finger and flew up and away, circling higher and higher into the sky. I felt as if it were carrying the weight of a long winter with it, as if I, too, were stretching my wings and letting Earthly concerns just fall away. The tiny creature represented so much about spring – the retreat of winter; emergence into a new phase of existence unbounded by walls and closed windows; the seeking of new light – longer by day, warmer by night and expansion into spaces bursting with new growth and possibility.

Of all the kind people I know around this globe, only a few others share a respect for the otherwise reviled stink bug. Considered by the masses to be an invasive pest, it joins the ranks of plants, trees, creatures, other insects and bugs who are thought only to be worthy of eradication. And the stink bug mostly draws ire from humans for its strong, pungent odor. But in my experience over many years, the odor is only released when the creature is injured or afraid – not out of malice, cruelty, or revenge. These traits seem to belong to the human species.

Those close friends who share my respect for the stink bug and other such creatures, plants, and trees, speak privately of their feelings. One person tenderly carries spiders outside; another the ladybugs; another nourishes the spindly, awkward little tree starts, giving them a solid fighting chance at survival. But it seems to me it is important to speak out about reverence for life – all life, as Dr. Albert Schweitzer did so eloquently. Because if we don't, even if at first no one listens to us, how will others ever consider *all* those who share our planet as worthy of respect and honor, of giving them a lift up into a life well deserved?

The other day I was behind a car with a slightly fading bumper sticker. It was in the shape of a ribbon and inside were the words: "I Love My Mutt" and a heart encircled the word, "Mutt" - extra emphasis of a deeply felt emotion. The sticker had obviously lived long on that car, but the sense of unconditional kinship shone strong.

Balance and harmony are also important and yes, some species are becoming invasive, the stink bug among them. But killing them as a means of control is not always the only option; often it means learning how to work *with* those who do take over, so that balance and harmony can be achieved. Australian author Michael Roads relates the story of how Wallabies were overrunning his cattle field, all but destroying it each night. It occurred to him to stop shooting the Wallabies and offer them a compromise – if they would leave the center part of his field alone he would give them the outer perimeter to graze on. From the moment he offered this (not at all sure it would work), the Wallabies never strayed out of the perimeter and his cattle could graze on an untouched field. There are many other accounts of people doing the same with insects in their gardens with great success, and my own experience moving field mice out of my house one summer by offering them safety in the barn. And, in each instance such compromises have worked, because the ground from which such balance is asked for, is respect for all life.

When respect, honor, and humility are the attitudes from which humans work, amazing things happen. Sometimes our own safety of course is important as well – no one recommends approaching a rattlesnake or lion with outstretched hand! But this does not preclude our attitude toward them as fellow residents of this remarkable planet.

I know of one person who said the stink bugs ate her garden one summer. She, by her own words, "hates them" and sets traps for them. That was the same season I released many stinkbugs back out into the spring air and not a one was ever seen in our vegetable or flower gardens nor have they been since. It does give one pause to consider another possibility.

Surprise!

SPRING GARDENS HOLD MANY SURPRISES. You may think you have laid out your beds and rows, followed all the rules for crop rotation year to year, picked out the best plants at the nursery, studied and practiced companion planting for the most efficient bug and weed control, and diligently prepared the ground with the finest combinations of manure. That all done, you sit back in satisfaction, sure everything will follow accordingly to produce the optimum harvest at the precise time appropriate to normal plant schedules. Or not.

In *our* garden, the first surprise was a tiny, newly sprouted seedling along the inside edge of a flower pot which last year had held a red bell pepper plant. But this was no red pepper, even though the first tentative leaves were a lovely crimson color. Within days our guest's identity was obvious –and astounding: a red Japanese Maple tree. The seedling had been carried on the wind from the tree in the front yard, clear across the house, to land in the dirt in the pot which still sat inside the vegetable garden. What a journey the seedling had taken. And how delighted we were, Michael and I. Together last year we had planned, built, planted and harvested the garden and while the Maple was not intentionally added, our guest was more than welcome. We prepared a place toward the back of the garden safe from deer and tenderly transplanted the seedling to its new in-ground home, then watered and tended it daily with encouraging words. I placed a little ceramic angel next to it for added protection.

Potatoes went in next, then onions, lettuce and cabbage, all in new beds full of rich compost from the donkeys, grass clippings and dried leaves. The strawberry bed, established last year, put out new runners and flowers, and by early May new fruit was forming.

Mid-May, Michael was watering the garden when from the strawberry bed he heard a loud and frantic crying. Something strange and furry was hidden beneath the mass of leaves and with brief, careful investigation we determined it to be a nest of baby rabbits. Spring Garden Surprise Number Two had declared itself. Quietly and quickly we backed out of the garden while a mother rabbit watched anxiously nearby. To our astonishment, she melted effortlessly through the closely woven wire fence and disappeared into the nearby brush.

In the meantime, our beloved garden was offering new surprises. Lettuce plants from last year's wind-blown seeds began appearing in other beds: one in the soon-to-be pepper bed; another in the gravel walkway by the garden gate; another in among the onions. This one had inspired a carrot from last year to re-grow. Potato plants began springing up in their old bed, now given to the peppers, right along with the renegade lettuce. So much for order and rows and rotation. Obviously the garden had its own plans.

We carefully avoided the garden for days. Thankfully, rain came frequently so our presence was not required. The mother rabbit was often seen hopping from the strawberry bed, around the bales of straw (for mulch), into the adjacent potato bed, and back into the strawberries.

Then one day, less than two weeks later, no sign of the mother rabbit. Perhaps the babies were out of the nest and on their own? But a tentative visit to the garden proved otherwise: three tiny bunnies with inch-high ears huddled together out of the nest, but under the strawberry plants. Time to retreat – again.

Days later one bunny was out of the garden itself, playing in the grass. Now they were, truly, out and about, mischievous, joyous bundles of boundless energy. The garden was ours – again.

But another surprise was awaiting us. While neither the mother rabbit nor her bunnies seemed interested in dining on the strawberries, lettuce, or cabbage, the one tasty bit was, apparently, the little red Japanese Maple – chewed to oblivion in one delicious bite. Heartbroken, Michael and I pondered the fate of the little maple who had made such an incredible journey, only to end up a rabbit's treat.

But the garden has offered us another surprise. For after contemplating the dire event I realized (Michael has yet to agree) that true to the nature of any garden, the Maple has merely continued its journey in a new way — quite wonderfully taken a step on its eternal quest, first with the help of the wind, then the pot, then us, and then the mother rabbit, surely a team effort, even down to the little ceramic angel who kept careful watch.

So what is next for the garden? I guess it will be a surprise.

Tree Folk

RECENTLY, A STRANGE CHANGE HAS come over me and I am not going to complain about it. It seems that my usual tendency to anxiety and fretfulness has calmed considerably. Not that I'm yet to the *Whatever* stage, but acceptance of things as they are appears to be my predominant reaction these days. I attribute this to the trees.

Ancient Celtic spirituality revered and honored the trees for their innate wisdom. Oaks were especially admired as great and wondrous beings. Native Peoples refer to them as the Tree People. Those non-Western philosophies that find sacredness in everything and everyone respect trees for their great patience and ability to absorb and transmute the toxins in the air. Some even say trees breathe for the planet.

An enormous triple-trunk Maple tree stands right outside my office window and while she lives on the property of our neighbors, I have always felt a great fondness for her. The tree company that carefully limbed her one winter estimated her to be at least three hundred years old. She's seen a lot of history; I do wish I was fluent in Maple and could ask her questions. What I do feel from her is an enduring sense of strength and peace. In my more frantic moments over the 39 years we have shared space, I have often turned intuitively to her silent presence for a greater sense of stability.

And, of course, my beloved Paradise trees that sport a canopy are perfect nesting places for squirrels and larger birds. I personally find their intriguing shape of both trunk and branches to be a lovely complement to the more native hardwoods and evergreens. Paradise trees are sturdy, rarely lose limbs in a severe storm, and hold their ground.

But pines, especially Virginia pines so common here in the Blue Ridge Mountains, topple easily with a bit of ice, heavy snow, or strong winds. Over they go in a heartbeat, their entire root system pulled out of the ground, often taking down fence lines or blocking the road. I always mourn the loss of the pines and wondered why they would have such a shallow root system and only one not-very-strong tap root.

A recent severe storm dropped heavy wet snow that took down power lines, brought enormous limbs from even oaks and maples crashing to the ground, and uprooted pine trees as if they were toothpicks. Our small acreage lost over twenty trees – all pines, and they lay piled one on top of the other, just as they fell.

After the storm, as I walked through our little forest I noticed birds everywhere hopping among the downed boughs. Chattering and singing, they picked at pieces of pinecone. A few squirrels gathered bits of broken branch in their mouths and hurried off to build nests. I expected to feel sad, to mourn the loss of my trees, but instead I felt as if there was a celebration of sorts – a release, a stepping forward with everything in perfect order. Brush piles would emerge later on to be safe homes to rabbits; bark would be consumed by deer and my donkeys, and eventually even the tall, now prone trunks would become mulch for the forest floor.

No longer did I see devastation, I saw beginnings – and more: a re-circling of life from birth to release to re-birth.

I surprise myself by these feelings because I am certainly one to worry and mourn. I have always been a saver (or attempted saver) of anyone injured, abandoned, or otherwise in need of assistance. As a small child I rescued bugs; six decades later my efforts still include bugs and countless other creatures, human and otherwise that form a very long list in between then and now. Not in my nature to say, "Oh, how lovely..." when anything is down and out, trees included!

But the forest is teaching me well and while I may still fret mightily when someone close to my heart is in crisis, I will also remember what the trees tell me, that life is not so much about physically surviving, but the gifts given along the way – whether it is a hand-up to another, shade from a tree's canopy on a hot day, safe haven in home and heart, or a bit of pine bark for a springtime nest: Life continuing, even when one comes crashing down. I can now see tiny leaves unfurling on my Japanese Maples....

Everyone Needs Lunch

A BIT LATE IN THE day for lunch, nonetheless I sat on the couch to eat my cheese sandwich. I would have to eat quickly if I was to get back upstairs to work on my book.

Jonathan snuggled down in his bed on the floor next to me; Snowy jumped up onto the couch beside me, nestling her head against my knee. Dog company can sometimes be the best kind to have any time of the day or night.

As I ate my sandwich, I read in one of my favorite books, *It's Easier Than You Think*, by Buddhist meditation teacher Sylvia Boorstein. She was talking about lovingkindness and how easy it is to love everyone, to wish everyone happiness. I set the book aside and sent loving thoughts to the entire world. It *was* easy; I didn't feel rushed anymore.

I was nearly done with my sandwich. I peeled off the crust that had some cheese on it, broke it in two and offered it to Jonathan and Snowy, each eagerly accepting their treat. After all, everyone needs lunch, whether it's a cheese sandwich shared, or loving thoughts sent out to the world.

It's really all just nourishment.

From Ember into Flame

"MY DEAR, YOU POSITIVELY GLOW!" my (honorary) Aunt Dorrie used to say to me with such enthusiasm when I was a child. She would tell me that my smile lit the skies and she could never get enough of it. Truthfully, what she saw standing before her was a child with a crippling lack of self-esteem, one who didn't fit her mother's expectations, lost without a father, and bursting to just be herself. But Aunt Dorrie, looking deep within me, saw my spirit and called it as she saw it. She made me feel better about myself and I adored her for that. And so thanks to her wise and compassionate ways, the light within me would, indeed, then switch on, although I wonder if I actually glowed.

As far as we know, everything on Earth is basically pure energy.

The properties of physical matter are complex: among them are minerals, water, cells, nano-particles. DNA and other things we aren't yet aware of. Big Mystery.

But what of spirit/soul? Not to be ignored, even somewhat by science these days, "it" can be a rather ambiguous term with slippery definition, not able to be measured or weighed or detected by the five physical senses, and open to various interpretations depending on one's own philosophical, religious, or mystical leanings. And the harder one does try to define the soul, the more indefinable it becomes. More Big Mystery. Needless-to-say, the scientific community has a tough time with soul. But for the purpose of this book, I would venture to say soul is the motivating, energizing, and creative force that *helps* shape and enliven any and all physical form. And to make this all the more interesting, I will add into the category of 'Form' all those also considered so-called inanimate (including but not limited to stones, clouds, water, fire, air, mountains, chairs, pencils, houses...). If you are still with me here, I will boldly offer that:

Within the center of every being (and thus every physical form down to the tiniest cell, nano-particle, neutrino, quark – well, hopefully you get my point), is light. Every single cell that composes you and me contains a photon of light and on this science does agree. But much like Soul, is this particular photon, or particle of light really beyond definition? Certainly it is not the same as the light we see by, at least with our eyes. This particular light can only be primitively described as a brilliant but not blinding point of illumination that is, perhaps, the infinitely capable motivating spark of life itself, *pure conscious and sentient* energy with its sole inclination to join the will of its physical host – human, animal, tree or otherwise, and spread outward beyond time/space as it is fanned into flame and offered willingly to others. A single photon; who would have thought it possible. More Mystery.

Confused yet? Think of a candle sitting in front of you. The potential of the candle is always there, but you must choose to strike a match and light the candle – and then its flame illuminates the room, maybe shines out of the windows and brightens the outside as well. But whether you actually see the illumination of the candle beyond the immediate area, the energy of that light travels much further than your line of sight because you can't contain energy, it must flow, and so, it will. Simple physics with a twist of mystical interpretation!

There are so many ways to feel that light within ourselves, to fan it from its glowing ember state, and offer it out into the world. It may be the kindest, greatest gift you can give yourself and any other: lifting another out of harm's way; being fully present for someone who is grieving; smiling at an exhausted postal worker at Christmastime, straitening and bracing up the bent stem of a flower, acknowledging the life in all things and acting accordingly with respect and appreciation for them, being gentle and forgiving with yourself when you feel out of sorts. Or finding that one thing – as with Lillie and the vacuum cleaner, Calliope and her many pillows, or standing under the stars – that sparks the light within you and sends it out into eternity. The list is endless, adventurous, and lovely.

And, paradoxical as it seems, fanning that inner light and sending it outward can also come from challenge, loss, pain, illness, or any of the difficult situations that present themselves. They, too, show us the way, give us a means of turning within to the light that energizes, motivates, and sustains us – if we acknowledge it and allow it to shine. How often have we been inspired by another's struggle against adversity? Or gotten through our own seemingly overwhelming circumstance and found *yes, we did it!* We can pat ourselves on the back – it's okay, because by doing so we are lighting up the world with the light we have found within us.

En-*lighten*-ment, or fanning our own inner ember, is not

complicated, difficult, or painful – ever. The flame never diminishes or goes out, so you can always find it. It is absolutely free – no paying back, no fees, no expiration date: it never goes away. There is no "deserving of it" or "not deserving of it" – there is no right or wrong attached to it, no level of spiritual attainment needed, no workshops to attend to find it. It cannot harm you; it is pure consciousness, ready to respond instantaneously to your request – verbally, or by your thoughts or actions. It will never let you down. And finally, it is environmentally friendly. A Mighty Big and Wonderful Mystery.

And also: Glowing Donkeys

DECEMBER 21ST. DEEP WINTER, FRIGID morning - ice left by a recent storm shimmered from trees, grass and fence lines. Bundled tightly in my heavy jacket, tall boots, and wooly gloves, I crunched across the frozen ground toward Nori and Julia, their thick, chocolate brown coats puffed out against the wind. For being such vocal donkeys, they were unusually silent, simply standing still in anticipation of breakfast and the arrival of dawn.

Sunlight arrived first, topping the Eastern Blue Ridge, spreading out and down like butter melting through the tree tops. Shameless sun worshipers, Nori and Julia lifted their heads to meet the approaching rays and bent their strong bodies into the welcomed warmth. And didn't it feel grand.

Even for December the sun is strong these days – Global Warming? Climate Change? Call it what we will, something is different from when my family and I first came to Virginia in 1978. Now, in 2018, I can hang laundry out on a forty-degree day and it will dry; there are places where the grass is as green as in spring, and the water buckets don't stay so frozen. This particular day, the sun pushed aside the sting of the early Winter Solstice morning with blessed determination, illuminating everything it met.

Including Nori – she was glowing! Sunlight enwrapped her

as if she were one of those lighted Christmas reindeer people put on their front lawns. But she also seemed to be illumined from the *inside*, the light pouring from within her, outward to meet the sun. Like cloud-to-ground lightning, where electrical energy rises from the Earth to meet electrical energy surging downward, forming a bridge of light between sky and land.

But it's easy for donkeys to glow – unless abused or neglected by their supposed care-givers, they are warm, delightful, loving companions to anyone fortunate enough to know them as I do. Stubborn? Of course. That's their job description: sturdy, strong of body and will, loyal and affectionate. It's a package deal; glowing is included. What a bargain.

But beacons of light with empty stomachs need sustenance just like everyone else, and getting back to business I distributed breakfast to my two sun-wrapped friends . As they ate, it seemed to me they were glowing just a bit brighter.

My self-esteem is barely improved over that of my childhood, but I have the memory of my beloved Aunt Dorrie to remind me that deep within my spirit I, too, "positively glow" just like my donkeys, and absolutely everyone, everywhere: human, tree, creature, plant… no one excluded.

Pin Cushion Wings

THERE IS NO DOUBT THAT our lives are full of edges. Some are small; we can easily navigate these, move on to the next event. But some edges are enormous cliffs- despite our best efforts we find ourselves pulled forward to the very precipice that threatens to send us plunging over into the dark and deep. What we've been told is that when we find ourselves teetering precariously, toes clutching that sharp rock beneath our feet as it is crumbling away, if we just let go, we will fly.

It's a great thought, but sometimes it just does not seem possible. I recently dropped headlong into the darkest valley I had ever encountered and not only did I not spring a pair of wings to get me out of there, I hit bottom with such a crash, I really did not think I would ever even stand up and walk my way out. Oddly enough, though, I did, in the most unusual way.

There really seems to be only one sure guarantee in this life and that is that it is temporary. But I also believe that even if the physical body crashes, the essence of who we truly are – soul, spirit, however one wishes to define our Essence – is *always* safe, always does have the wings to fly, and eventually will indeed fly out of here. But not before our share of edge-walking, cliff-plunging, near-drowning in grief (please excuse the cliché), and that persistent pile of fearsome boulders called despair, frustration, anger, doubt, severe loneliness that tend to crush, bury and otherwise pulverize us all too frequently. You know, all those dreadful feelings that pour over us and make us want to shout aloud, *"Enough already! Why bother trying anymore?"* and ending with – *"I quit!"*

And indeed, why bother. Go ahead, cave in, give up, roll over and put your paws in the air. However, here's my story about four little neglected and abandoned pots of Blue Pin Cushion plants who showed me a different way.

In the first six months of 2014 I learned some new things about pain – hard, crushing physical pain. A cyst had apparently taken up lodging in my lower back, and with its continuing enlargement, bore down without mercy on the nerve bundle that comes down the spine. It was powerful pain, I couldn't sit or stand, lying down was tenuous – only walking gave any relief and after a while, one just has to stop and rest. I reached the edge of that monstrous cliff, fell off, didn't fly, but did – finally – have surgery to remove the offending growth. Recovery from the surgery was long and discouraging with its own bumps and setbacks, and I often wondered if I would ever be well again. I had, as a result, given up. I felt weak and useless, had no interest in going out, eating, reading or writing. All those things I love to do were gray, flat, unappealing. Only my animals, children and garden gave me any joy. Six months of misery had not only knocked me straight off the edge, but bent into disrepair whatever wings I might have sprouted, or so I thought.

But sometimes those wings come in strange forms and despite circumstances and our despairing emotions, they will find us and lift us up after all.

Two months post-surgery, I wandered half-heartedly through our local garden center. Usually in the back of the store are a couple of tall carts with shelves full of mostly dead, dried up, tossed-away plants at bargain prices. With just a tiny bit of curiosity left in my tired mind, I walked back to take a look. There I found several small pots of one of my favorite perennials: the Blue Pin Cushion plant. And they were, indeed, nearly gone, not unlike the way I felt.

I leaned into the shelf and studied them. They had not been watered, left for dead. I found four that while truly pitiful, seemed to have just a few strong, dark green leaves at their base. The flowers were dried and brown, barely a hint of their normal gentle blue selves. Marked one dollar each (truly a bargain), I gathered them up and carried them tenderly to the register.

The woman behind the counter looked at me for a moment with curiosity – was this customer really going to pay four dollars for these sad specimens? But I had faith in my little charges and I was not going to bow to anyone else's opinion. Without realizing it, quite possibly this was the first sign of "wingage" sprouting – that lifelong fierce loyalty to underdogs rising in my Celtic soul once again.

At home I placed them in the kitchen sink and gave them a thorough and loving soaking, reassuring them they were now part of the family and after a night of rest in the dogs' garden out the back door, they would find freedom for their roots in my peace garden. Seriously pot-bound, I could almost hear them moan, but with the promise of release in the morning, hope was indeed on the way. They had plunged off their cliff and found their wings. Me.

I lifted them from the sink and set them on the kitchen counter and carefully pruned back all the spent blooms. A few new green shoots tentatively poked up through the soil. I encouraged and adored them, told them they were so beautiful and perfect and that they were, finally, home.

In the morning, as promised, I planted them in the little garden dedicated to all those creatures who have graced my life, brought me back from the edge of many cliffs, and given me wings to fly onward again. In reflecting on each of them, I realized my four little Blue Pin Cushion Plants had not come to my attention by chance. Had I heard their call? That faint, ever so slight nudge, the whisper that is so easy to miss? But *I hadn't* missed it! My heart took me in their direction and there we were. Four half-spent plants stuck on a bargain shelf and one struggling human just wandering through a garden center had found each other.

So as it turned out, they were my wings as much as I was theirs.

It's spring, a year later, and we're all doing splendidly now.

Getting Specific

I JUST KNOW SOMEONE IS standing just on the other side of the veil that separates dimensions, holding a clipboard with my name across the top. Guardian angel? Spirit guide? Maybe, or Personal Coordinator, Director of Operations, Liaison for All That Is. Not that I ever see or hear this particular entity, but he (or she) has a certain presence that can't be denied and I've grown so used to that presence, I wouldn't want it any other way.

Working with said entity can be a learning curve – no one passes out a manual, DVD download, or even as much as an inter-office memo. Still, there certainly seems to be some kind of coordination in communication efforts. For example:

Many years ago, when I had 10 dogs and a variety of other species under my care, I was feeling pinched financially. What to do? I addressed the Quantum Field of All That Is (QF for short) in the middle of my living room, on a Tuesday, mid-morning. *Please send me abundance,* I called out into space; *Right now, I accept abundance!* I announced to the ethers. Positivity, declaration of wants and desires – that sort of thing.

Right-o! The one with the clipboard replied, not so that I could hear, but turning to the next in the chain of whatever command there may be on the other side of here, sent my request full-speed and – early the next morning a new very small, very homeless dog was sitting on my doorstep. *Not that kind of abundance, guys!* Or, One Human's Crash Course in Getting Specific. It all worked out anyway: the little fellow with the white ruff around his neck, just a pup, became Dog Number 11, or Emmett Alexander, and enchanted us for thirteen years. Still.....

There are times for daydreaming – letting the mind meander around without destination, and I love these times, like a Sunday road trip into the mountains or five straight days on the calendar with not a single appointment marked on it. And sometimes it's good to just stand in the living room and *suggest* to the fellow with the clipboard: *So what do* you *think my life needs right now, another dog? Maybe start a business? Plant some exotic tomatoes?* And see what comes up. It might be none of these, kind of a grab bag of possibilities. There does seem to be a rule attached, however – that fine print at the bottom of the form*: Leaving things up to the Quantum Field means you can't complain about what you get. Oh, and P.S. – The QF has only your best interest at heart.* Or, to paraphrase: Everything always works out for the best (more on this later).

I've seen this happen, and I've seen getting right down to specifics happen as well. For instance, whatever benign force keeps sending me heart-shaped things, does seem to be looking out for my best interest. Truly now, how can one find anything but affection in a huge heart-shaped puddle, or a tiny piece of avocado in the shape of a perfect heart, smack in the front of my kitchen cabinet?

Sometimes, however, said benign force seems to be off on vacation, or taking a nap because suddenly where there were daily, sometimes multiple daily hearts, there are noticeably, none. And right about the same time, something dramatic shows up in my life that is definitely not joyous. When my world stops shaking for a moment, I usually remember to, yes, stand in the living room and ask, *"May I please get another heart-shaped something?"* And guaranteed, by day's end, there's a perfect heart-shaped stone at my feet, or certainly by the next morning a chunk of toast falls onto my breakfast plate into the shape of a crispy, cheerful, buttery heart, or I feel compelled to look up and there in the sky is an undeniably white, puffed out, heart-shaped cloud.

Thank you! I always remember that part, even though it's not in the fine print that I have to. And that doesn't mean my life suddenly gets bright and shiny and perfect – in fact, I often have a long way to go before I hit bottom and start back up. But I have a heart-shaped something to hold close and help me climb and the reassurance that the being with the clipboard is still with me and paying attention.

Getting specific is akin to the Buddhist practice of mindfulness, paying close attention to the moment so that when I am then sending the request (not a *demand*, understand) my attention remains on the object of my request rather than sidelined to all the quibbling arguments my brain may be trying to throw in the way:

I need to restructure the barn, re-roof the house, build on a small room, get some decent work boots, pay off the credit cards, go to the dentist, make some donations... $250,000. Please.

And then the little Quibbles show up: *You don't really want to go to the dentist, do you? If you redo the barn, you'll disturb the birds nesting in there; okay, pay off the credit cards, that would be good, but you can get by with sneakers from Wal-Mart....* And my friend with the clipboard is saying, *So, what is it, $250,000. or $9.95?* You can see how mixed messages can mess up the bottom line.

There is that old and very accurate saying, Be careful what

you ask for, because you will get it. So I've learned to do a bit of both: really know what I want and get down to specifics, and also, recognizing the greater wisdom of the QF, add: *Or whatever you think is best for the greater good – my own (and thank you) - and of all that is.* And I just know whoever is "out there" sending me hearts, has written on that infamous clipboard:

Not to worry, we're looking out for you! Thanks, you guys.

Saying *Yes* to Trees

IT'S TAKEN ME FIVE DECADES to finally learn how to stand up for what's in my gut. No, not all the intestines, but that surefire means of knowing if what I am feeling or about to do is appropriate or not. You know, that famous "gut feeling" – good equals calm; not good equals pain, right there in the very center of the stomach or solar plexus. At least for me, that's where the center of my intuition seems to reside and it has never misled me.

The first ten years of my life I was very good at saying no to others, mainly to my poor mom who had to deal with her Irish-tempered independent child. But once I hit that turbulent eleventh year, suddenly what others thought of me began to take precedence. Would my friends not like me anymore if I didn't bow to peer pressure? I believe I was about twelve when my then friend and cohort, Candy, convinced me to try smoking my first cigarette in her parents' bathroom. I hated it right away, but didn't dare say so. Candy was rebelling against her new step mother; I was just along for the ride. Smoking that first cigarette started me down the path where one tends to only listen to and follow the clamor and chatter of the world at large. And of course, paying attention to the world is important, after all, we are born into it and must live within it. But there are other options as well; I just needed to remember them.

When I was in my early 60s, I started realizing I was wearing down. And a good place to start rebuilding was by not trying to please everyone simply because I did what they requested. I'm a tender soul and don't like to disappoint anyone. To be truthful, I also want everyone to think I'm a good person. But change was calling loudly to me, too. Maybe it was my gut, or maybe it was the trees.

All my life, from infancy on (or so my mother told me later) I have always listened to the trees – and the wind and stars and water and plants and animals…. Earth, herself, in all her completeness. Even in my "distracted" teenage years, those of the natural world whispered to me, even if I didn't always hear them. But my mother listened to trees as well and all those not of human form, seeking the Mystic's path and encouraging me to do the same. There, she continually reminded me, I would reconnect with my soul and spirit, find my roots and much like the trees, learn to stand firmly connected to the Center while reaching outward and upward to the light.

Many trees rise from small seedlings deep in the dark soil. As they grow year after year, sometimes century after century, they speak silently of strength and perseverance, bending into the gales and storms that lean against them, and ever offering shelter, shade, and nutrients, returning all to the Earth that gave them birth: the circle of life; the Center of all Beingness. Acceptance. Generosity without thought of return. Resiliency. These are the strong, heart-centered lessons that would never fail me.

And so I resolved to once again, as I did in childhood, listen to trees, to answer their call to follow their ways with *Yes! Here I am!* I quiet that worldly chatter; I go and stand with them and give them my complete attention. And they respond in kind. How reassuring to know I never have to please them or could possibly disappoint them, mystics that they are.

When I stand or sit with trees, even in those times when I can only do so sitting quietly on the couch in the late afternoon, I find indescribable peace. It's the same feeling I have when that inner voice – call it intuition, gut, whatever – firmly tells me the direction I need to go, what is appropriate behavior or timely action. I feel loved and comforted. Do the trees and my inner guidance system have a secret line between them, somewhat like when as children, we played telephone with two tin cans and a piece of string? I know I do not hear the trees through my brain or ears; their "voice" is soft, intangible, but sure, and lands so perfectly in my consciousness like a bird settling on a thin branch. And it is the same with my intuition – it's just there, landing precisely, definitively, leaving me to find my balance and acknowledge its wisdom (always a good idea) or conversely if I *think* I know better, and charge off in a different direction (never a good idea).

The other night I had a dream about a tree. As I stood under her, looking up her 100 foot trunk in love and admiration, she leaned down and embraced me. Clearly, she was an extension of Mother Earth herself, for she, in turned, wished only the best for me. And so it is with my intuition, even if it means politely saying, "No, I can't" or realizing a decision I am about to make is not the correct one. My intuition wraps me in its warm arms and like a responsible and caring parent reminds me of another way, but never makes the choice for me.

The morning is moving on; I have to clean the barn, fill water buckets, hang out laundry, check email. But something within my inner gut is pulling me in another direction, and while I know all those practical tasks demand my attention, I will lay them aside for just a while and heed the call of my beloved trees.

Finding Light

CHRISTINA (MY ENSPIRITED COW) SAID: *And when you're sad or tired, just go back to the light wherever you find it; I'll always meet you there.*

Deepest winter, just past Solstice, minus five degrees with the wind chill. Normally in such conditions I would be bent over, head down as I trudge out to the barn to tend to the donkeys. But today, remembering Christina's message, I am seeing light everywhere. Not so hard to "go back to..." if one knows that no matter how dark and cold things may seem, there is always light to be found. And I've been looking.

The deciduous trees have shed their leaves; daylight and moonlight flood through bare branches, illuminating the air, reflecting back off the ice on ponds, water buckets by the barn, frozen patches from yesterday's rain. Ice particles in the garden's bird bath send sparkles outward into the curly, dried remnants of last fall's perennials, even off the asphalt shingles on the roof of the house.

A crow silently wings his way above the field across the road, the deep purple/black of his feathers shimmering in the chilly air. The front lawn wears a coat of frost; above me, the sun declares our return journey to the core of our solar system.

Sad times, exhaustion – is there anyone not familiar with these points of shadow that appear to block light in our lives, when it can feel too dark to find our way back up and out? Just been there earlier; it has not been a great morning for me. But now I consider what Christina said and I find even just the tiniest point of light, a spark, and it changes everything for me. There it is, that same spark of light in the eyes of the animals: my dogs ecstatic to see me when I walk back in the door; gladness in the demeanor of small birds as I put fresh seed in the feeders; a bit of white quartz – heart shaped, as if glowing at my feet; stars in a cloudless night sky – the Andromeda Galaxy overhead; the last star before dawn; the first star at dusk; sunrise, moonrise.

Night comes early this time of year. People feel depressed – not enough light. But that's when I can close away the busy obligations of the day and go within, find the light in my heart. How?

Perhaps it's through prayer, meditation, or contemplation. Perhaps it's through reflection on those of all species, kindred souls who have, by their very presence been a radiance in my life. Sometimes it's one word, a passage in a book or a phrase remembered; a song or a story.

But what about those times when none of these work? I'm just too tired, discouraged, in too much pain to even consider finding light – in my environment, internal or external. I'm just a pitiful heap of despondent human scrunched up on the sofa hugging my pillow.

And that, invariably, is when the light finds me – my sweet, soft dog, Snowy, nestled next to me, laying her head in my lap. Or Emma, wild princess of a magnificent feline leaping across the back of my chair announcing "Here I am, head scratches, please!" Or something/someone unseen nudges me to look up to the photograph of my beloved Christina looking out at me from her favorite room in the barn. And I have to smile, it's involuntary, it's the opening door that allows the light entry.

And then I recall Christina's words, and her words remind me that the light is always available, always here, *knows* me, *loves* me, finds *me* – light that is as alive as the air I breathe and the ground I walk upon. And in that space/time of unwavering illumination within my heart, I do understand this, only sometimes – well, I just forget.

So, Thank You Christina, and *all* of you who help me remember that light abounds, I only have to turn and see it. May we always find each other there.

Bird on a Post

HE SAT ON THE FENCE post, puffed out against the cold and in no hurry to go anywhere. He looked forward, only occasionally tipping his head to one side or the other. Cardinals whizzed past him on the way around front to the bird feeders; a crow, lifted high on the air currents, crossed above him, and fellow robins hunted for old seeds on the ground below him. But he didn't move, his dark eyes blinking rapidly, taking in the world from his elevated perch.

A Bird's Bird, he exuded self-confidence, calm, and satisfaction with how his life – at that particular string of moments – was shaping. I watched him for a long time, ten minutes, perhaps, and not once did I see him take out a smartphone and text anyone. If he had a scheduled meeting he was not rushing off to it; nor did he follow anyone on Facebook or Twitter. If he had gained weight over the holidays and his feathers were feeling tight, he wasn't mentioning it, nor was he offering any opinions on politics, religion or immigration. He had no notion of or interest in sales events, close-outs, or stock reports.

His consumer's footprint was minimal: he had no possessions and left no trash. He was, in fact, exquisitely Environmentally Correct.

I loved his posture: upright on two tiny, twig-thin legs; perfect balance, perfect symmetry. Obviously for his own well-being, his vision was sharp, focused, all inclusive of his surroundings. He missed nothing. When you are prey you can't get lost in filmy dream-states or mindsets that churn the past or imagine the future. Pointed, present, receptive, he was a totally complete package of poise, elegance, simplicity, and beauty.

Tomorrow this magnificently appointed creature might be food for another, but even so he would leave behind a silent message of immeasurable value just by being himself.

I took one picture of him, sure that he would then fly away. He didn't, I took more. The more I studied him, the more he became iconic of everything I admire and struggle to become. Without yoga classes, shamanistic workshops, intensive weekends, tele-classes or e-books, this robin, balanced on a fence post on a chilly February day, had all the natural wisdom within him – offering it freely through living demonstration to anyone who chose to notice. And I did, gratefully. I lowered my camera and bowed to him. The honor to be in his presence was all mine.

What Can You Show Me?

IN A SINGLE STONE THERE is the miracle of life – not just the life of today, the breathing, walking around, being young and smart-alecky, getting old and wise kind of life, but the whole span of *everything.* Take a stone in your hand and close your eyes. In silence ask, *What can you show me?* What, then, do you "see", do you sense? Perhaps it will be boulder, once thrown high and far from the heart of a seething volcano, or a mass of red-hot, fiery-white, molten lava, coursing down a mountain of ash to the forest or sea.

Or was it born eons ago *in* the sea, composed of the tiny shells of once-vibrant ocean creatures, layered with sand and silt washed down from high mountains by rivers and streams? What monumental force of nature drove those sedimentary layers up and out of that sea, then tilted them to form new mountains, craggy cliffs, boulders, and single stones?

Stone holds the secrets of the Earth, her passage through her own life and evolution and the secrets of all who have, do, and will reside upon her. But Stone is silent until it breaks loose from where it has clung to for so long, and then, in its forward journey roars pounding, echoing as it tumbles on.

Or silent until you sit in gratitude, and ask, *What can you show me?*

All the while Stone, in its journey, is creating Future, not just for itself, but for Earth, for all of us. There is the wearing down to sand and soil, building ground for others to take root and grow. But more: Stone shows me what it is to have strength and courage, singleness of purpose, to accept evolution with grace and the interconnectedness of all things. I have opened my mind to this "being" and asked to be shown, and more new worlds than I ever guessed existed reveal themselves to me, worlds that have been, and those yet to be. And piercing all those worlds, holding them together, dearly, like the petals of a flower is the answer I seek.

It is the same with stars.

I can look up on a moonless night into endless bright clusters and single shimmering orbs. Awestruck, I imagine what it is like to run among them, to catch the sun's light as they do, and reflect it back to everyone else around me. They are *light* years away! My brain can't count that high, but I can let my mind bend the borders and pretend I can. To think that what I am seeing now, is already perhaps thousands if not millions of years old by the time it reaches Earth.

Then mid-day I look skyward and see only blueness and the passage of clouds. Where are the stars? Have they "died" and gone away? Do they no longer exist? But I know better. Obscured only from my vision by the visible sun they still stand waiting. Are they themselves looking down on me, sending their history forward, outward, into the past and present?

And I ask the stars: *Are you dreamers, too?*

I sit on the floor beside Sophie, my old, blind terrier. I know she will be leaving soon, dropping this physical shell to rebound into the fullness of timeless/spacelessness as her ancient, spirit self. As I stroke her soft wheaten colored coat I can only imagine her puppyhood, for she came to me already advanced in years. But her cells hold all her history, not just that of "Sophie," but of all her selves: past lives and those yet to come. Where will she be? Who has she been? And will our lives intersect again, in some other decade, country, century, world, eon, galaxy? Will she and I sit together dreaming with stones or run chasing one another through fields of stars?

I believe the possibilities are endless.

My Sophie rises, stretches and yawns and I help her walk stiff-gaited outside to relieve herself. We are two "people" touching our feet to the strong earth, tending to business, being very present and aware of one another. And we are two souls who have been/are/will be the perfect mix of old friends, so comfortable with one another.

Too grand, like the stars, like the stone to possibly "die" and never be again!

I have only to ask with complete respect, *What can you show me?* And a single stone in my hand, a sky full of stars, and a dog in my heart give me the most important answer of all:

Everything and anything is possible.

Key for a Good Laugh

SOMETHING MADE ME STOP ON the path as I took a walk through our woods. Instinctively I looked down and there by my foot was a small, angular rock, almost a triangle. Intrigued by the shape, I picked it up and turned it over in my hand. Where the rock was widest, at the top, was clearly a face – two wide round bulgy eyes and below it a V shape cut in the stone that ran from edge to edge and looked like a great big grin. I smiled back at it, put it in my pocket, and continued my walk.

Back inside the house I took out the small rock and set it up on the kitchen windowsill, the face facing me (excuse the pun). It really did make me smile – a great wide grin of my own.

But being in my philosophical, mystical mode, I wondered what the significance was of the stone and my attention being called to it. (I have long since learned such events are not random or accidental.)

In my mind I heard the word, "Ki".

Ah, I thought wisely, *Ki – yes, the Japanese word for energy, how profound!*

I detected a chuckle in the atmosphere around me. And the following:

No, silly. No Ki, Key, for Keystone Kops!

I looked more closely at the grinning stone and laughed. Of course! Rock with a sense of humor – old fashioned, classic – and if you have never seen an episode of the Keystone Kops, you might want to, because it will make you laugh and no matter how sick or tired or down you are, you will feel much better. Created by Mack Sennett in the early 1900's, the Keystone Kops films are terrific silent slapstick comedy. (Clips are found on Google – be sure and look at the episode, *The Keystone Kops Meet Pickles and Pepper*.)

So Key still sits on my windowsill, reminds me to be cheerful, and that even Earth can have a great sense of humor.

Being Fragile, Growing Free

Two SMALL GRAY-AND-WHITE BIRDS HAVE built a tiny nest in the crook of a lower beam in my barn. Barely six feet above the ground, the delicate nest is a work of art: woven green moss amid strands of golden hay. It is not the typically round shape of a bird's nest, but as if a bowl tipped a bit on its side, it is higher toward the back than at the front.

For weeks now since the nest first appeared one morning, I have been witness to the parent birds – so shy of me – flitting in and out of the barn, first to lay eggs, then to set, and finally, with nestlings emerged from miniscule white shells, to raise their four young ones.

I have worried endlessly about them. They are so close to the ground and there is a neighborhood cat on the loose. Then also the nest seems so precarious, tipped that way – I have to continually remind myself that the parents know what they are doing. And the babies: their eyes are still closed, but they have tiny wings and tails and gray fluff on their heads. Each day their cries are more insistent when the parents arrive with fresh tidbits for them to eat.

They seem so fragile, I said to the donkeys this morning as I spread hay outside in the sun for them. For the first time I was aware that I was equating fragility with danger, certain loss, possibly perishing at the hands of a cat, or a fall to the floor before. All very negative, uncomfortable images. There had to be another way to look at this state of being and so I began to think on the concept of being fragile.

"Pull yourself up by your bootstraps and be a good little soldier," my grandfather used to say to my mother when she was a child. In his opinion there was no place for tears or weakness, she would tell me, partly with sorrow, and partly as a parent now herself, to pass along such a strange (to me) philosophy. She once remarked with pride that she never had shed tears, even in her darkest moments. She was tough, strong, presenting the brave front to all she met.

Inside, however, she – a remarkable artist, writer, and lover of all life – was so very fragile. Apparent to others, she, herself, never realized this until in her early 80s her long-term memory returned and pain from her childhood years often brought deep sobs from within her. Of course she is gone now, so I cannot ask her, but I wonder if it was not the very fragile nature she maintained throughout an often difficult lifetime, even though buried deep within, that helped make her the magnificently mystical and spiritual being she was.

We always hear about people with incredible strength and courage and rightly so, we applaud them. They overcome the toughest obstacles even though beaten down again and again by whatever force challenges them, be it their own health, another person, political system, or society-at-large. We raise these people high on the heroic pedestal and swear to be more like them ourselves.

But what about the fragile ones, like the butterflies who live such short and tenuous lives? I watched my son, Tim, labor tirelessly to carefully free a swallow tail butterfly from the front grill of his truck and then with a silent blessing, set it free. Together in awe we watched it soar into the luminous purple blooms of the wisteria on the garden gateway where it fanned its paper-thin wings before flying up and away.

And there are the clouds – never the same in shape or form one second to the next; how fragile they seem. Perhaps to the human mind their "lives" are unreliable and unpredictable. Yet we admire them as they shift and gather and drift and evaporate or pile high into storms only to be chased on by encroaching weather fronts and brilliant sunsets. Perhaps if we more closely admire those who are fragile, delicate, and vulnerable we can see in them the uncompromising value of living more closely to the numinous, holding the wisdom to move on from physical life with grace and ease. Like the delicate sky-blue Chicory blossoms that last but a few hours to fade before the sun, or tiny fledglings balanced so precariously in a wisp of a nest, do such ethereal beings reminds us to walk more mindful of Spirit and a Greater Sense of Things?

If so, I suspect their very fragility will remind us that we cannot, nor should not, hang onto anyone or anything; we cannot make anything survive in the physical world no matter how hard we try. And that is really all right, as it should be in a world shared with Spirit.

As I finish writing this two days later, two of the fledglings have flown free of the nest, winging high with their parents in the nearby trees. The other two also flew, but out of their bodies to continue their journey into the Light: all four fragile – all four free.

Green Leaf (and Thunder)
Social Media

THE LITTLE CLOVER SPOKE TO me – I swear she did: "Don't step on me, please!" Right there where I cross the backyard to the donkeys' fence, one footstep away. I wasn't looking down, goodness knows I wasn't listening for small voices, but there it was, I heard it as clear as anything, more like an impression lighting up my mind. Instinctively, I pulled my foot back and looked down and there "she" was, one of most beautiful, perfect four-leaf clovers I had ever seen. Facing up to me. Fragile open leaves waiting for the sun, so vulnerable. I leaned down in admiration, thanked her for calling out to me, and placed a rock beside her to remind me of where she was. I wished her a brilliant day and continued on with mine.

It was not the first time I have been called to by those traditionally thought (by modern Western Society) to have no voice or mind, let alone soul or personality. After many decades of such encounters, they no longer surprise me. The trick for me is to not be so locked up in my own thoughts that I don't hear them.

Years ago, while absorbed in a TV program, suddenly there was a tiny, faint voice in my mind – "I'm thirsty!" it said. I looked up to the top of the TV (those were the days before flat screens) and there was my little potted germanium. I got up from my chair and checked the soil and sure enough, it was completely dry. The little plant looked droopy and desperate. I quickly brought it to the kitchen sink and gave it a good soaking, reviving it in time. I've been more mindful of my plants ever since.

One December afternoon, I was driving Michael and Tim home from school down our country road. We talked happily about our plans for Christmas. For a reason I could not understand I began to be enveloped by an immense sadness, and a non-physical pain flowed through my entire body like gray smoke. I was compelled to focus on the pickup truck in front of us and there in the back lay a smallish, freshly cut pine tree. I was feeling the despair of that tree; there was no doubt in my mind. I sent it thoughts of release and peace and the grayness began to ease. Starting with that Christmas, we have never had a cut tree since.

I am by no means a professional Communicator – with animals or anything else, despite my lifelong desire to be Dr. Doolittle. When the messages come, they come unbidden, slicing through my often overly-practical, busy mind. Those animals who have managed to cross my brain barrier, do so when I am not looking to connect with them; and they have been, for the most part, creatures living with me, many who have died, and in two distinct instances, dogs who were on their way here but had not yet arrived in my life, letting me know they would be joining our family.

I am delighted when I hear such messages, and it humbles me to remember that we are all part of the community of life, no matter our shape, species or age, even the "unlikely" ones: mountains, rocks, thunder.

Not a fan of thunderstorms, I do, nonetheless, respect their power and acknowledge their place in the scheme of things.

Thunder Beings, I call them, in Native American tradition – sentient "peoples", fellow citizens Earth's natural world. And when they are bearing down on my home and barn, I address them directly, asking them (hopefully) to please move away.

During one particularly fierce storm that seemed fixed over us, I hid in the bathroom (before I knew that is *not* the place to be in a storm) with five rapidly panting, dogs, all equally as anxious as I was. Convinced this storm was going nowhere soon, I began chattering nervously to the Thunder Beings in an attempt to distract my frantic mind.

"Thunder Beings," I began shakily, "Please go around us – please take your wind and lightning elsewhere; please do not harm us!"

Instantly, there was a sound in my mind – clear, strong, and oh, so unexpected. It was as if the storm itself had gone silent and all I heard was the sound which said:

"Harm? What is 'harm'? We do not know what that is."

Two things occurred to me very quickly. One was the shock that someone had actually heard my plea and that 'someone' could only be the storm: Begging by Rita; Reply by Storm. And then that these towering, thunderous potentially life-taking beings had no concept that what they were doing wind and lightning-wise could cause destruction. *Nor did they have any concept of destruction or harm.* The storm was simply being itself, following the laws of nature. The rise and clash of hot and cold air currents. The storm had *no intention* of causing pain, loss of property, maybe even loss of life. For the storm (and I would venture it is the same with all of nature including earthquakes, tsunamis, sandstorms, Derechos, volcanoes etc.) did not equate what it was doing with anything but the natural physical patterns of the planet.

I really had no idea how to answer the storm's question, how to define harm, but the incident changed the way I will always look at such potentially critical events. I do remember thanking whoever had answered me, for being aware of me and my concern. And if such beings as storms can push through *my* chattering brain, surely they can reach just about anyone, opening vast doors for intercommunication and cooperation. We just have to believe in all possibilities. Then paying attention is a good, and a respectful thing to do.

Long ago I gave up trying to find reasons and rationale for such events. Each one reminds me that magical things happen all around us, intriguing things that only make life more interesting and profound. It's kind of like Social Media – you get to meet all manner of new friends and share in what they know. My four-leaf clover and I now "like" each other, our own version of Facebook, but better, because I get to be outside in the natural world rather than in front of a computer screen, and my clover plant continues to thrive. A pretty good deal for us both, in my opinion.

Life, I Love Your Face

ROSIE, I LOVED YOUR LITTLE face and everything about it: that black wet nose surrounded by white whiskers; your honey-colored coat that fell in wisps around your ears and flopped down across your forehead like a little shelf. I loved the way the far ends of your mouth bent, emphasizing that fierce eight-pound terrier spirit that earned you the nickname, Rambo. And such determination in those ever-on-guard eyes! I loved the feel of your fur against my fingers and the way the top of your head fit in the palm of my hand as if your head and my hand were made for one another. My Rosie: I loved your little face, Dog's-Face: adoring, protective, trusting and always glad for everything. I will always remember it.

So many faces to notice, to love, to look into deeply and know there is only oneness between them and me. Take Christina, my once-and-only beloved bovine: your broad pink nose covered in bits of grass; intensely dramatic white eyelashes that eased down with every slow-motion blink of your enormous dark eyes. The wide, sloping brow and boney point right at the top of your skull, covered with "feathers" of hair that were soft and clean. Your strong jawline for chewing cud; the sweet aroma of your auburn-and-white coat, like Crayola Crayons or the graphite in a freshly sharpened pencil. Christina, I loved your big broad face

– Cow-Face: steady, centered, focused, and serene. And I will always remember it.

There are other faces, too. Everything, everyone anyone can think of has Face: birds and insects, flowers, fish and amphibians, even mountains and oceans, sky and clouds, the Earth we walk upon. I love all the faces, reflections of the life that surges throughout the adjoining form: creature, plant and tree form, land form, my form and yours.

That little triangle of granite who so politely corrected me that his name was "Key" for Keystone Kops - still sits on my kitchen windowsill and I often say to this little piece of stone, *"I love your face!"*

There is the face in the moon when she comes to full. Can't you imagine she is blessing us as she looks down on us here, on her companion planet, grateful for our company? Moon's Face: so content, motherly and protective.

One warm June day I found a praying mantis on the fence-post. As I admired the long green insect with the folded hands, it deliberately moved its head and looked directly at me. The large black eyes turned down slightly to quizzically study me, this two-legged member of the inferior (human) species standing before it. I was appropriately humbled. The mantis' gaze was so profound I had to finally look away, at which point it turned its head back forward and in no hurry or fear of me, left my company.

We "face" things: adversity, the wind, our fears and doubts, courage for whatever we feel life is throwing our way, or at us. But does life also have a face? Are there ever-changing, expanding and contracting expressions that keep me moving forward when life is wide-eyed and active, charging ahead with me barely hanging on by my fingernails?

I know that life can then change expression – gentles, encourages me to rest when everything is slower, maybe even nearly still, nothing much to stir the waters, so-to-speak. Life's face reflects the pulsing rhythms that make it what it is: creation and re-creation, ever shifting waves and particles of energy. Perhaps life's face is broad and strong. But there is also a bony outcropping on top with a peak that is soft and clean, one to climb up to hand-over-hand and look around at all the world offers.

As I choose to look deeply into life's eyes, I see my own soul reflected back to me, and then I look further and see the soul's face of all beings everywhere as inseparable from me – all those faces I love so very much, the big ones and the little ones, each one unique and so very wonderful: dogs and cows, cats and trees, stones, clouds, rivers and mountains, humanity, all so incredibly beautiful. Faces I will always remember. And I have to say:

Life, Thank you - I love your face.

Small Wonders

I SAVED A SPIDER TODAY – one so tiny that at first I thought she was just a bit of dust blown by a puff of air. This always seems to happen when I sweep my sun/plant room; spiders, ladybugs, stinkbugs get swept from corners to end up in the dustpan, careful and watchful as I try to be. Patches of sunlight, interrupted by the shadow of geranium or petunia leaves, confuse my vision and so I have learned to scan the dustpan intently before dumping its contents into the wastebasket. Thus, the spider, seen only by her almost imperceptible struggle to free herself from her current predicament within the swept up old flower petals, dried leaves, and dirt that had fallen to the floor. A tedious task, being watchful for these delicate creatures, studying those sweepings until my eyes cross. But it is just part of my job – no bug too small, that's always my motto.

This particular spider-being re-defined "tiny" - the wee-est creature I think I have ever encountered, outside of perhaps a gnat. Reaching for my designated, well-used piece of old business card, with utmost care I raised the spider to the safety of a nearby plant, one with pink blossoms, where she scurried off out of sight. Later I found her spinning a new orb-shaped web as if nothing out of the ordinary had just happened.

What I marvel at is that such a minute creature functions so perfectly by the order to which she belongs, being 'spider', no less aware of her task and purpose than say, the elephant or whale. Different parts and size, I grant you, but still – there is movement, intelligence, instinctive drive that keeps 'my' spider doing what spiders do, controlling other insect creatures who wander just a bit too close. In someone as tiny as a speck of soil, or the point of a pencil, just think of the parts held within, and how those parts all work together in perfect order, as our parts do for us, as all of nature does, down to the seasons, phases of the moon, rotation of the planet, the rise and fall of the tides.

It's just plain awesome.

So what is the Intelligence behind all the miracles called bodies, minds, dare I say souls – in fact, life itself? Yes, I dare! I cannot imagine my tiny spider does not, *is* not, soul personified, when everything else is in such immaculate order about her and within her. And, my only and immediate response to seeing her struggling to be out of danger and back to her known world, is to help her – person reaching out to "person" of a different species, shape, size, form, but nonetheless, one in need of compassion, honor and respect. Soulwork, for both of us, spider and human. Soul (mine) met Soul (hers) and in some unfathomable way, we both are changed in a beautiful, positive manner, at least so I believe.

Conversely, had I been repulsed by her presence, glad for her entrapment, anxious to destroy her and then done so, that thought/action, also, would have changed us both, and perhaps because we are all energy, changed the entire universe, even if by a very small fraction, but in a negative way. So say the ancient mystics and now, so say quantum physicists.

I thanked that tiny spider for the crossing of our ways today and apologized for having disturbed her. Perhaps it was meant to be. If we do, indeed, share the same field of energy, then she knows my intentions were honorable, and on some mysterious level I have yet to understand, we will remain connected by a silver threadlike connection not unlike her own spider's silk, as we each busy ourselves with our individual lives.

I would like to think that Earth turns a bit brighter for our encounter.

Dreams Sky Blue

SETTING OUT PETUNIAS IN THE Dogs' Garden, I was particularly entranced by the opalescent purple-blue blooms that cupped around a center of yellow and white, deep in the heart of each one. With tenderness I patted fresh soil around the new little plants, gave them water and a blessing. It was only then that I noticed the small plastic tag with planting instructions – and this particular kind of petunia's name: *Dreams Sky Blue*.

I sat back on the grass and contemplated the magic of such a name while my dogs charged joyfully around me, stopping occasionally to stand on back paws and lick my face, or scrunch close against me for reassurance of our absolute and mutual adoration. What could be better than this?

Dreams Sky Blue – what a wonderful phrase to carry with me, to balance everything in my life upon: limitless, perfect, uncluttered dreams of all I could ever desire.

And in the heart of each desire, a clear center of yellow/white.

I watched my dogs chasing one another and realized I already had so many of my dreams right here, firmly grounded in physical reality. Home and family, a small sanctuary for creatures, ancient, blue-green mountains at my doorstep and all their wildlife, even the occasional black bear. Even more: excellent friends, the kind you can entrust your life to and never worry that they will turn away. Good books and music, goldfinches at the bird feeders, my own keen and curious mind; my wonderful donkeys, cats –

And my dogs.

Beyond that ring of the Blue Ridge Mountains, I thought, *the world rages on – war and hunger, greed and fear, all the frustrations of trying to fit into modern society, our so-called 'civilization.'* As humanity is drawn in ever-demanding, multi-tasking, often opposing directions, where is the time, energy, or common sense even, to sit back and allow for dreams and visions, without guilt that we should be accomplishing something, making better income, being more productive, making a name for ourselves, texting someone!

Dreams Sky Blue.

Such good advice from a garden nursery. I had my own pitfalls, no doubt about it. And one particular writing project loomed higher and more demanding than just about anything else in my life at the moment. But yes, if I allowed my mind to float in *that* direction, I could easily cover that Sky Blue with the densest of thunderheads called stress. But instead I closed my eyes and mentally cleared the clouds away, allowing the crystalline blue to once again fill the sky of my mind. Endless, boundless, limitless. What *would* I dream or envision if there were no limits to my success? I opened my eyes and stared into the azure summer sky above me and as if like soft cloud-forms, I pictured everything that I would want, for myself, for those I love and admire, for everyone.

Dreams Sky Blue.

What fun it was to send my dreams and visions dancing upward into the atmosphere! And encouraging. Anything and everything is possible I've heard, and so I now believed. Then

Snowy, my sweet, soft-coated Dandie Dinmont licked my hand and Jonathan, my wooly miniature black poodle scrunched close to me. While Lillie, my lovely little Shih Tzu raced in ecstatic circles around the maple tree.

And so, looking skyward I continued envisioning everything I love. And right then, most especially my dogs.

More Friends,
Human and Otherwise

Now, MAYBE MORE SO THAN any time in our known history, modern-day humanity is coming closer to a consciousness that respects and honors all who share this planet: every species, every form, and recognizes that everything, even that which may be classified as inanimate, contains energy, life and spirit.

I offer here just a few of the countless people who have so positively influenced my life, have been my supreme teachers especially during my early years, although there have been many more throughout my seventy years.

And, those we call "objects": words on a simple invitation, a special chair, a car among others – unusual teachers, I admit, but worthy way-showers none-the less. I do believe there is wisdom in a stone, a single drop of water, a mountain range, an ocean and so much more. The ancients knew all was alive, felt companionship with all around them, and acted accordingly. As we step forward in time, are we actually reconnecting with a brighter, wiser time?

Bella and Miranda

EVERYONE I KNOW NAMES THEIR car. My '99 Honda is Bella the dragon-mobile: sturdy and strong, dependable and my friend. Her paint is a dark royal blue with sparkles throughout, her tires are deeply treaded, balanced and aligned. And despite her nearly 200,000 miles, she never misses a beat going down the interstate, over the mountains, or through city traffic.

If only human beings would be as fabulous.

I really do also know some tremendously fabulous people – and I don't mean to come down on the human species. It is my own after all. But rare is the man or woman who does not insist on giving well-meaning advice that has not been asked for, or offer opinions that would best be left unsaid. Or play politics or missionary. Or heap on guilt as if it were a woolen blanket. As I sit here contemplating what I have just written, I can readily name twenty good (really good) friends who are as dependable and gracious as my car. When I try and take the list further, I start to drift.

My house has a name: Miranda, although she also could easily be Bella, which means beautiful. An extraordinary dwelling, Miranda is much more than just a house or structure, but a *home*.

Home takes the concept of a place to live to endless depths of love and affection. These are the instinctive feelings I have for her – after all, for almost 40 years she has, without complaint, sheltered myself and my family of humans, animals, plants and my ever-growing rock and seashell collections. Windows and glass doors throughout with skylights in the roof make her appear to be as a crystal, even at night when the lights are on and I am standing outside, admiring her. She welcomes and embraces all who come through her door without judgment or hesitation. But then, she is no youngster – her original part being built nearly 90 years ago and the "new" addition in the 1960s. So she has age and wisdom on her side, as well as experience and mellowness of character. And what a foundation! Stick-built on a fieldstone base, framed in real wood (no composite, thank you). In other words, Miranda has substance.

Both Bella and Miranda are graceful, simple beings – not fancy or modern, no complicated, state-of-the-art anything or expensive adornments inside or out. Both do their jobs well – transporting or protecting, giving all who live or travel within a view to the outer world beyond glass or open window, clear of commentary or self-pity.

I consider all of this as quite a gift given by what most people would consider A Car and A House. Not me. Just as for so many years the animals and human friends who have shared my life have given me so much, so have my home and my dragon-mobile shared so unselfishly of themselves, and in return I do my absolute best to keep them clean, healthy, and loved. Now, if I could only emulate them in *all* those other fabulous ways as well, a singular way to honor all they do for me, to let them know just how very grateful I am. I have a feeling they already do.

With Regrets

AN INVITATION TO A FUND raiser dinner arrived in the mail today. Enclosed were a return envelope and a small card with two places to check off my intention:

I will attend, bringing ___ guests.

I am unable to attend, with regrets.

And a place to sign my name.

The invitation came from an organization with which I was only vaguely familiar. I did not wish to attend, and I had no regrets about my decision. Yet, I was not offered the option to simply say, *Thanks, but no thanks.* For some reason, I felt cheated of that third option. After substantial fussing and self-pity, I remembered that declining an invitation with regrets is merely a formality, quite acceptable in higher social circles. My circles don't expect regrets, and invitations are usually by email, a conversational exchange between friends, or a spur-of-the-moment decision to have a gathering. You know the kind: "Hey! Why don't we meet for pizza at..." But the stark white card with embossed black print on the table before me, did get me to thinking about regrets – what that means, and why it might be best to banish the word and gesture entirely. It is, after all, not very positive and seems unnecessary to me.

Christina, my beloved Hereford cow stepped on my foot and it really hurt. I asked her to please lift her foot, she did, and we both went on about our day, I limping, she chewing her cud. No regrets were forthcoming. Oh, I guess it could have been a different scenario. For example, I could easily have had regrets for not paying attention, knowing how she often lifted her foot to shake off flies. And, Christina could have regretted putting her foot to mine, causing me pain. Had any of this been the case, we might well have spent the afternoon apologizing profusely to one another, feeling sorry for ourselves, and each other. But that did not happen. We survived the incident and left no trail of sad and pitiful regrets.

Calliope, ever the hungry hound, would scour through Emma's litter box in anticipation of finding a solid gift left by said feline. In the process, she scattered litter everywhere, tracked it throughout the rest of the house, and never looked back...with not a regret in sight. Moving on, she would find a sunny place to sleep, I would sweep up litter and the day continued. No one can train a hound so there was no reason for anyone to have any regrets.

Regrets, to me, are synonymous with hand-wringing, sweat on the brow, prolonged agonizing over ill-made decisions, or words spoken in haste without forethought. Truth is, we all make mistakes, some minor, some pretty big. As one who, admittedly, spends far too much energy exclaiming "I am *so sorry!*" I can assure you not much is gained by doing so. If the recipient of my apology is a person, more often than not they feel obliged to reply, "Oh go on, don't be silly!" Or if my sentiments are directed to a flower, plant, tree, or animal I have in some unintentional way caused distress or pain, the response, without exception, is always - silence. It would seem the one in question has already moved on to the next moment. Those of the natural world are proficient at doing so. I am learning to follow their lead.

Do I regret choices I have made in my life? Of course, we all do. Does regretting those choices change anything? Nope. Am I a better person because of my regret? If I have learned from my mistakes then the answer is: Not in the least. I have found that a wiser choice than regret is simply to say to myself or another, "Oops. I could have done that differently; lesson learned."

I feel that regret is like a black hole in space: you can get sucked in and lost in the process. If and when you emerge, you are never a happier person for it. So like all black holes in space, or in our minds and emotions, best to just avoid them altogether. I acknowledge the situation, tend to it in a positive and loving manner, and move on. Works every time.

The invitation on my table? I simply wrote in my best handwriting: *No Thank You.* My intention clearly – and politely – stated. I'll mail it back tomorrow and head on into a new day.

No regrets.

Significance

THIS MORNING I HAD ONE of those delicious moments of instant realization and it involved the word and concept, *Significant.* Honestly, I had never thought about how often I use significance in defining and compartmentalizing things and other beings in my life until this morning when the meteorologist on the news talked about "A significant weather event" on the West Coast, and there I was, coffee cup in hand, sitting straight up and taking notice. Not about the aforementioned weather event, but of a piece, if you will, of myself that needed tending to. That's how these A-Ha! moments happen for me – if I am actually paying attention to them, they are great teachers and wake-up calls.

On this particular morning I realized that, as (to my credit) is a quite normal human habit, I often mark my journey through life by what I do and do not consider to be significant events and other beings, even clues for trying to solve one of the many puzzles confronting me, what I may decide to be a significant piece of information in my own healthcare, for example. By definition, I consider to be significant that which stands out for me in the ongoing flow of eternal existence as it carries me along, Sometimes, I admit, I differentiate, or judge one thing as being more significant than another, and can even minimize something or someone as *in*significant, not worthy of my full and focused attention. By the end of the newscast that went right on without me, I was actually feeling pretty down on myself, not the intention, I'm sure, of whatever prompted this most recent draw on my thoughts.

I decided I needed to change the direction my mood was going, and because nature always cheers me up, I walked outside and stood in the sun. For a November day, the air was unusually warm and everything around me in garden, sky and trees was unhurried, brilliantly dressed in color and sound, inviting me to be a conscious participant in what was truly a beautiful day. I breathed slowly, deliberately, easing my entire sensory system – physically and intuitively – into the progression of fluid moments with no divisions of time or space.

What I was experiencing was without doubt *significant* to my pursuit to be more fully aware of and an active participant within Essence, oneness, flow, and energy. But there was my brain, once again attempting to define my experience. I asked to see this differently, from a much broader viewpoint. Silence. I was trying too hard to hear an answer. And then I was distracted by a tiny, brilliant red ladybug, climbing along a stem of dried grass and immediately I realized that everything is significant – down to the tiniest of miniscule atoms and bits of dust. Even what is generally considered mundane, such as washing dishes or cleaning the cat box is significant. Everything, *every one* of every form, color, shape, species- seen and unseen – everything in the ever-present moment holds significance, is significant, has its place and purpose in the overall flow and inter-weaving web of life, for the very reason it exists. Nothing more, nothing less. All that is, has significance.

I walked down the driveway to the road, collected the mail from the box, and started back up, checking to see what had come: the telephone bill, a credit card statement, some advertising fliers...my mind automatically dismissed them into "useless, for recycle" and "important – don't lose! Needs my immediate attention." I stopped in the middle of the driveway and sighed. Looking down I began to really see what was around my feet – newly fallen leaves, bits of tiny stones, fragments of dried flowers and seeds in lovely patterns enhanced by the black pavement beneath them. I continued my walk back up to the house, opened the garden gate which caused the small wind chimes hanging there to ring, answered by the call of a White-throat sparrow by the garden pond as water cascaded down the rocks, sunlight tucked within the ferns along the pond's edge....

Looking around me, I could not see or hear or sense one single thing that was not alive, was not significant to all I am, to all we all are. Even as I looked at the bills in my hand, I realized their significance – due payment for services that made my daily life work smoothly. And I felt grateful.

Now how can that not be significant?

"Deliciously intense, Surprisingly balanced"

THESE WORDS ARE NOT MY own, but found in tiny gold print on a Lindt chocolate bar, *Supreme Dark*, no less. The chocolate, once consumed, was delicious (and healthy, 85% cacao) and the words written above, once digested into mind and soul: invigorating, reassuring, and thus, absolutely health-supporting (100% inspiring). Which brings me to the Animals' Peace Garden where I live and thrive, and what it is basically about. A personal story seems appropriate here.

Christina, my Resident Queen (and only) Bovine, had a "situation" which required the good services of my large-animal veterinarian, Dr. John Wise. Since Christina was no one's dumb-animal/ fool, Dr. Wise and I had a certain routine that needed to be adhered to if he would be able to treat her. Because she knew the sound of his van as it turned up the drive, she had to be already secured in her headgate, or chute, about ten minutes before. To this end, Dr. Wise would call me as he turned onto my road to let me know he was about 10 or so minutes away. Sometimes it took two people, much maneuvering, and blocking off of possible retreat points to coax her into the chute because she remembered, and what she recalled were neither pleasant nor soul-fulfilling activities. In a few words, she had a malignant tumor in her right nostril (from ultra-violet exposure for her 16 years) and securing her enormous head and treating the tumor were not activities she would have voluntarily chosen. But, one does what needs to be done. It was okay. She was a tough girl and Dr. Wise and I were determined care givers.

Dr. Wise is a pro – gentle, considerate, and skilled in getting the job done quickly and completely. Of course, none of that was appreciated by my distraught creature and once the work was done, options discussed, and she was released from her confines she would march a short distance, stop, turn her head towards us, and if looks could kill…. Well, you get the point.

It was one of Those Days, nine a. m., an October day cool and clear. Perfect. Mission accomplished, Dr. Wise and I shook hands and he was on his way and I continued with my morning's tasks. Christina begrudgingly finished the treats I had set out for her, then made her way down-field for her morning nap. After a while I walked down and leaned over to speak directly to her. "Thank you," I said with genuine appreciation, "for being so helpful and easy to work with. We all consider you a very special cow." She looked at me with slightly dimmed eyes, clearly her message being "Whatever. I'm not done with this yet; check back with me later. Bring food."

As I patted the top of her head and walked up toward the house, out of the corner of my eye I saw she was once again chewing cud, head stretched out in contentment. All had returned to How It Should Be in her world, in her own mind. No grudges, no self pity. She was done with it after all.

There is a quote I particularly love and read often: "Peace," the unknown author writes, "It does not mean to be in place where there is no noise, trouble, or hard work. It means to be in the midst of those things and still be calm in your heart."

In the *Animals'* version of a Peace Garden, one learns to deal with the hard places of life whether pain, predators, difficult situations, perhaps grief for someone lost, and still move forward. I have learned by paying mindful, respectful attention to those of the animal, tree and plant kingdoms, and certainly thunderstorms, that fear is not the overriding sense/energy of these beings. Instead, it is moment-to-moment acceptance of things as they naturally occur, with no frustration, resentment, anger, bitterness, plans for war, or revenge, compulsive comfort food, or shopping. Life just as it is, moving on. And when the difficult things happen (such as veterinarians and head gates or painful joints on damp days) one does what needs to be done, *and yet, also* is always ready to return to peaceful ways and times. The heart knows they will come and how to find them.

Animals are not lesser beings, they just have no sense of being entitled and so, no desire to linger in their pain, physically, mentally or emotionally. Seen this way, life *can* be deliciously intense, and yet, in the realm of Nature, likewise surprisingly balanced. My (finally) contented Queen Bovine always proved it so.

Fire! *Or,*
"Please pay attention..."

I HAD GONE TO MY friend's house to bring him some groceries. He was a kind fellow and offered me tea. At 84 he was housebound and enjoyed the company. He brushed off the one chair facing the old sofa. Cat hair of the most interesting colors and felt mice with bells attached, fell to the floor. He offered no apologies, knowing already that I am an animal enthusiast.

Cats were everywhere: huge, furred out gray cats, slim black cats with watchful eyes, affectionate ginger tabbies and three white ones with blue eyes. There were stoic, middle-aged cats and old ones, curled into circles, drifting in and out of sleep. My friend loved his cats and took good care of them. You could tell by the easy look on all their faces.

As we drank our tea, he told me cat stories. "Once," he said, "the man came from the gas company to clean the living room heater. That fellow kept looking at all the cats while he was fiddlin' with the heater, tighten a few bolts, blew dust out of the air intake valve. He seemed awfully quiet, not very friendly. All of a sudden he spoke what was on his mind.

"So I guess,' he says, 'if I want a kitten, I know where to come for one.' He was turning some knob on top of the heater but looking around the room. But quick and sharp I said back,

"NO sir! All *my* cats are fixed."

"This repair guy turned the knob on the stove one more time and straightened up; he was grim. And that's when fire shot up out the back of the heater. He got it out quick enough, but I could tell he was angry he had messed up. He didn't say much after that, just finished cleaning up the soot, laid the bill on the table and left."

One of the white cats jumped into my friend's lap and he laughed quietly.

"Sometimes, I guess it's just good to pay attention to what you're supposed to be doing."

Hanging Bells on Garden Gates

I HAVE A PASSION FOR bowls and bells. While I appreciate many material things, I hold few of them in the high esteem I do a round bowl in my hands or a string of bells on the garden gate. Here are two objects that may seem quite distinct from one another, yet they share one precious quality: they impart a sense of simplicity, clarity, joy and calm.

Bells and wind chimes soften the sharp right angles in my home, where wall meets wall: a clean, but unyielding edge that too often reflects those judgments, thoughts, and anxieties in my mind. I open one of the three gates here leading into a garden and there is the sweet clear sound of the bells – tiny cat-shaped ones on the front gate, a string of old brass Indian bells on each of the back and vegetable garden gates, and magically my brain stops its current rampage. Without effort, automatically I close my eyes and listen, leaving space for peace and joy to flood back in.

When I kept a herd of goats, all their collars had bells attached – some were bells from Switzerland, hand-painted with flowers and leaves in bright colors. Others were small brass bells, each one giving off a different tone. I remember the herd coming into the barn in the afternoons – I could hear their bells long before I saw them – one of the most beautiful memories I have.

Wind chimes also hold the same gifts as bells for me as I rush about my day: on the front porch, some wooden ones, others made of copper tubes, and those long, resonate aluminum ones… each set of chimes offer, in their own sound, an invitation to return to sweet balance and joy.

In the dogs' garden there is a young maple tree and from one of its lower limb hangs a set of chimes: two metal feathers tapped softly in the wind by a brass dragonfly. I found them at a discount store, fell in love with their design and brought them home. Now placed where I hear them even in the slightest touch of wind, their melody, sweet and subtle, is like an old friend touching my hand to remind me that what really matters is in the heart, like my dogs as they lie in the shade of the little tree on summer days.

I wouldn't be surprised if bells and wind chimes have their own spirit/soul, even perhaps distinct personalities ranging from the intensely deep ones to the tiny, crystal bells in the Buddhist temples in the Himalayan Mountains. But this is not just my theory. Mindfulness Meditation teachers begin and end their practice by *inviting* the bell to ring, a sign of acknowledgment and respect - for a fellow being? A humbling thought!

Bowls, likewise, offer solace and a return to centeredness when I hold one in my hands. One of my favorites is a small bamboo bowl given to me by my sister, Tao. Its exterior is a pristine, matt finish of robin's egg blue. Sometimes it holds healthy things for body and spirit: garlic bulbs, or wrapped chocolates (not at the same time!) and one October, dried marigold seed pods to be planted in the spring. But often it stands empty as well, ready and willing to be my cup of sky-blue peace and equilibrium.

Round bowls, so perfectly shaped, remind me that the universe loves a sphere – a drop of water, the moon and planets, the circle and cycle of seasons, night and day, sunrise to sunset. How we come back time and again to what we love most, whatever that may be for each of us.

When I am particularly stressed, if I hold a bowl in my hands, close my eyes and bow my head, I find myself embracing a great and generous teacher. The bowl may appear empty, but it is, in actuality, full of all possibility, it becomes my Quantum Soup bowl, not limiting or containing, but allowing all that possibility to flow freely within, through, and beyond the bowl, myself, and all the universes and dimensions no matter how far they extend into infinity.

And, sometimes, if I am really distraught, that little bowl in my hands, so perfectly balanced and light to the touch accepts all my current fears or grief, or anger, or despair – and while appearing, on the physical plane to have solid structure, its depths are, on a nonlinear, non-temporal level of existence endless, ready to take all offered it, within its heart without complaint or limitation. Everything, including my tears that I pour into it.

Not long ago I was in a store that sells many high end items, searching for a particular gift for a friend in California. While I admired much of their merchandise, being on a strict budget I yearned, but passed by, everything else on their shelves. Until I found a stack of very small, pure white, perfectly shaped ceramic rice bowls. I bought four, didn't look back, brought them home, and I could not be happier. Now, if the store had also sold bells – I probably would have bought them as well. Bells and bowls are, for me, teachers, friends, a hand up in an often confusing, chaotic world. My practical sense may stand aside for bells and bowls, but it is a passion I am happy to live with.

In Lieu of Thoughts and Prayers, Send Chocolate

I HAVE A GOOD FRIEND who almost always closes her emails with a reminder about the healing power of chocolate. So often we are corresponding back and forth about problems with our animals or other such gut-wrenching concerns; not long ago it was my husband's unexpected death. And while so many deeply caring friends wrote to me that they kept me in their thoughts and prayers, her determination that chocolate best soothed the weary soul confirmed for me that comfort and peace can also be found in tangible things that grace those five useful physical senses we carry around with us so close at hand, so ready to assist us.

Other people I know obviously share the same philosophy. Following Doug's passing, I received all kinds of physical gifts: deliciously fragrant hand cream; a small, magnificent crystalline glass cow I placed next to a berry-fragrance candle; a bag of freshly ground organic coffee; herbal tea; and a book about animal angels. One friend and fellow author sent me a poem she had written just to comfort me (knowing how much I love poetry) which I still read aloud from time to time, listening to the sound of the words as they flow around me. There were many more beautiful, tasty, useful, inspiring, joyous objects that appeared on my doorstep at a time when grief dogged at my heels and I could hardly find the Earth beneath my feet.

Tangible objects keep us grounded and centered, reminding us that *this Earth, this life,* this moment in space and time are equally valid and necessary to the care and nurturing of our spirit/soul as well as our body. There are no limits to the possibilities. This is not to say we need to clutter our personal environment with "stuff," but given or chosen carefully, the beautiful, the profound, the funny, the tasty, the fragrant, the inspiring can only round out in three dimensions what the fourth and higher dimensions of prayer and focused thought bring to one's greater and infinite Self.

When I sign a letter, card, or email, it usually is "With blessings, peace and love...." I would chose, if it were possible, to attach a bar of dark chocolate, a cup of hot tea or coffee, a tiny pewter angel, a heart-shaped stone or a fresh and fragrant flower. In other words, something to hold in the hand, to taste or smell and revel in the sensation; perhaps a small volume of excellent poetry to read aloud, or a CD of cheerful, foot-stomping songs.

Thoughts and prayers, blessings and peace, and most certainly love are excellent gifts of the heart to give another. *And* – a small, beautiful tangible "something" as well, not fancy, large, or expensive, but carefully chosen and sent for the joy it will offer. These, then, become ultimate treasures given from one heart to another, acknowledgement of the physical beings we also are, with an especially deep bow of respect to the power of chocolate.

Student Driver

TURNING ONTO THE INTERSTATE ONE afternoon I found myself behind a car with a large sign on its roof that declared, *Student Driver.* Seasoned drivers usually sigh deeply, expecting perhaps erratic behavior from the poor nervous kid behind the wheel, a bit too much hesitation on the forward motion, anxious leaning on the brakes, maybe even some weaving in the steerage. But the kid (or late-learning adult as the case may have been) has to be commended for getting out on the road and trying, not the easiest task when other cars, tractor trailers, SUVs, and gigantic motor homes are racing around and past them. Maybe giving the student driver a bit of extra room is precautionary, and one day that new driver, by then experienced himself, may do the same in a similar situation, but I think that giving any student a thumbs up for effort is a gracious and generous thing to do.

I can track back over the decades of my life the times that I, too, was a student driver not just of an automobile, but of major learning experiences I either chose, or life chose for me, to take on. And similar to that student driver in front me on the road, every time I would wade straight into each one as fearlessly as possible, and come out (hopefully) more skilled than when I went in.

In the depths of the process I would weave and wobble to find my balance, hesitate often, afraid of what might lie ahead or around the corner, and draw up in a sudden stop when I thought I had taken a wrong turn. Achieving my license to learn and live wisely hasn't come that easily. To name a few such times (and these really are the big ones, literally from the ground up): Learning to walk as a toddler; in third grade, staring through tears at the columns of three numbers I had to add up; high school, boyfriends, and learning Latin; living on my own in a big city in a new country; a challenging 41-year marriage; childbirth; raising teenagers (especially after remembering, with embarrassment how difficult I had been as a teen); caring for my aging mother who suffered with dementia after a major stroke; her dying and death; Doug's long unstoppable descent into deep depression, withdrawal, and eventual death; my own trek into long term, chronic Lyme Disease, Fibromyalgia and body-wide arthritis.

Each of these situations could fill a chapter to themselves, but taken as a whole, for me they represent to me a quest of sorts that is almost mythical in proportion: the knight setting out to find his or her true self through facing and conquering all kinds of obstacles, beasts, doubts and fears and that pesky reoccurring desire to just give up and go back, forget the whole thing because *it's just too much work.*

But of course, I didn't, and the uncertain student driver in front of me isn't going to either because built into each of us is that failsafe compass that reminds us we are, after all, made of tough stuff, we *can* do this (whatever it currently is) and, therefore, we will.

As I write this, I am not yet through the dark forest of chronic illness, the end is not in sight, and admittedly when the pain and fatigue overtake me I stop being so brave and wish I could turn back. But not for long. My Irish/Welsh heritage that makes me Stubbornness and Determination personified pushes me on, and besides, I have a plan.

You see, for any such major challenge, I think it is good to have a really wonderful – maybe even a kind of silly reward to reach for. Okay, your own motor vehicle driver's license – that's cool, I agree. After nine months of pregnancy and however many hours of labor – a beautiful child is hands down the best kind of reward. But for just about everything else that's really painful to struggle through, a good bowl of your favorite ice cream simply cannot be beat. Unless, of course, you are lactose intolerant, then you might want to consider just taking a day off and spending it in all the gentle, fun, and glorious ways *you* choose.

After all, life has just handed you your driver's license and now you can really get up and – *go!*

The Step-Aside

WHEN MICHAEL BUILT A NEW front gate leading into the Dog's Garden, he engineered a four foot by four foot square section just to the left of inside the gate, beside the walkway. He framed it in treated wood for durability and filled it with gravel. The purpose of this "step-aside" as he called it, was to provide a mud-free area in which to step after we opened the gate to enter the Garden which also is the most frequently used entrance to our house. Now a person could open the gate just enough to get through without letting dogs out, a maneuver that requires immediately stepping inside to the left of the gate. Before Michael's invention, there was a dirt patch there that turned to mud in the slightest rain, messing up peoples' shoes and mood. But the gravel, neatly contained within the wood frame, allows for shoes to stay clean, and for much less grumbling.

I wonder if we should construct a mindfulness Step Aside just to the left of the gate to each moment we experience. Imagine if we took one or two seconds, just long enough to focus our awareness on the experience we are about to enter or the words we are about to say. What if we would then pause at that threshold, open it just enough to not let out anything we don't want loose in the world (especially if we are about to "have words" with someone) and take the time to step aside into a clean space, and then move forward from there? Presumably, we would be accumulating and tracking far less of the mental and verbal mud that can occur, improving everybody's mood.

From time to time the gravel Step Aside needs my attention. This morning I noticed all kinds of growth poking up between the stones – morning glory vines, a dandelion plant, even some determined paradise tree sprouts. Left unattended, the Step Aside will soon resemble a small forest and its initial purpose and good use will be obscured. As I took note to clear the framed space, I listened to my thoughts – some rather tangled and weedy ones were poking up, without whom my own inner Step Aside could better serve *its* purpose of clear mind and clear heart.

Recently, Michael made plans for a newer gate, one not quite so large as the present one which does tends to drag on the walkway when opened. *A bit higher up,* he thought, an inch or two of ground clearance. Always wanting to improve on his ideas, he considered doing away with the Step Aside.

Gates are meant to open smoothly, whether physical or theoretical, so I applaud his new design. However, I asked him to please leave the Step Aside as it is – a good reminder for me to walk lightly – and easily – through the entrance to every moment. I can face many such gates in a day.

Hold, *then lift*

THE PLASTIC CONTAINER OF MIXED baby greens I buy has an extra strip of plastic along the front that helps keep the lid tightly closed. Inside, the lettuce, kale and spinach remain fresh, but opening the container can be a challenge and it must be done with care, attention, and patience.

On either side of the strip are the words, "Hold", imprinted into the plastic on small tabs. I have to look closely to see the words and beside the "Hold" tabs are two even smaller ones that simply say, "Lift". The words are very present and extremely helpful for opening the container, but subtle as well, easily missed if I am in a hurry to make my lunch or as often happens, my mind is distracted.

Inside the "container" that is my *Whole Self*, is abundant, fresh sustenance for the mind, spirit, and soul, exactly what I need and want in my life. But for much of the time my container remains tightly closed because I fail to listen to the clear and simple directions my inner self offers. Life on the surface can confuse and scare me. But when I can "hold", or quiet my distracted thoughts,

I can easily "lift" the lid to the vast world that lies within myself to access the contents: perhaps peace, happiness, ease of mind, openness of heart, courage, a sense of safety and joy.

And as I draw on what I find within myself, from the container that I am, I am always nourished.

The day as yet unspoken for...

ONCE, WHILE CLEANING CAT BOXES I wondered how it would be if upon waking up each morning, to give the new day a chapter heading. I often think like a writer, even during the most so-called mundane jobs such as washing dishes, hanging out laundry or as in this case, being somewhat deep into feline care.

Several years ago a phrase floated up and into my brain, much like those messages in the old Magic Eight Ball we used to play with as kids. I have no idea where the phrase came from as it was not connected to anything I was currently reading, working on, or even thinking about. But there it was, front and center to my conscious mind and I really liked it. And the phrase was:

The day as yet unspoken for, waits patiently before me.

Considering that each morning is akin to a new beginning and our lives are like unfolding storylines, why not think of the day as a brand new chapter based on two possible considerations: One would be what was already planned for the day, perhaps a trip to town, working in the garden, time at a job outside the home – our lives are certainly full of schedules and To Do lists.

But how about creating instead a chapter heading that speaks to how we would *like* the day to go – perhaps an adventure tucked in there somewhere, meeting a new friend or time spent with an old one. Easy, comfortable, lovely - the possibilities are cosmic.

In the plot of my life's ongoing story, since I am the lead character here how do I envision its direction, what is the scene I wish to set? I regard it as a mental exercise that is fun, but not something to become attached to if it doesn't work out.

You see, as any writer dedicated to his or her craft knows, there are times when you have followed all the rules of writing, carefully laying out your plot, and creating your characters, setting them all of in a certain direction formed in your own imagination. And then something strange begins to happen. The characters themselves start to tell the story quite on their own; the plot suddenly takes its own twists and turns, and you, the author, have become more of an observer and facilitator, a secretary as it were as the characters begin to live their own drama and adventure. It's quite amazing when it happens.

So what of my newly hatched day as I emerge bleary-eyed from sleep? I give my day, perhaps as yet unspoken for, a chapter name: "Not So Tough as It Seemed" or "A Grand Day for Cloud-Walking" – just getting really creative to spark the day. But I don't become attached to how it ends up traveling, maybe even in the completely opposite way from what I imagine. I don't allow myself to become frustrated or angry or sad as it takes its own course. Because from the phrase that came so mysteriously to me, the day, itself, seems to have its own spirit.

But what's interesting is that the more I do this little creative exercise before even getting out of bed, the more often now my new chapter title will illustrate how my day turns out. Am I, at the very least, the *co*--author of my own life? I have to wonder....

Halt! *(maybe)*

Speaking of intuitive nudges:

Vince, our kindly postal guy, handed me my mail; we talked for a while, he continued his mail route and I returned inside to pour my coffee. One-ten in the afternoon, still time for some creative writing *if* I could keep myself from being distracted. In my estimation, the day was still ascending.

My day starts early – five AM with the sound of braying donkeys out the back door; my best alarm clock. It's uphill from there: critters to feed, food to cook, dogs to walk, check on the garden – the list is long, and routine. Around noon I realize time is ebbing away – lunch, only three hours left now to work at my desk, then time to begin afternoon feeding, fill water buckets for the donkeys, bring in laundry, start dinner… in other words, the day has started its descent toward evening.

Since I am prone to stress, I then try to cram everything in as fast as I can until I am just too tired to make one more step. If, at five PM I can look back on my day and feel I have accomplished something not just routine, but constructive (working on my book for instance) I nod and smile and breathe normally – probably for the first time in hours. But if in my assessment I

189

feel I have achieved little forward motion in other than daily obligations, I start to ache and wheeze and fuss and complain – to myself, as the dogs, cats and donkeys are not really interested in my self-incrimination.

Nor are the trees, the squirrels, the birds, or the clouds.

I have wondered if any of these beings have hypertension and achy bones because they (the trees) did not: grow enough leaves that day; find all the nuts they hoped for by noon (squirrels, of course); do their cloud-job description of dropping rain here and there; and so on and so forth.

Hardly.

Unlike the above beings who stick to their true calling, be it leaf involved, searching for food, or forming around dust particles high up in the atmosphere, I, being *human* being, have mastered the science of getting distracted. Not once in a while, but on a continual basis. If I am going from Point A (need to water the plants) to Point B (then write two important letters) I carry my water jug upstairs to find the floor needs sweeping, this or that plant could use a trim, and there is Emma-Anne, my beloved cat, who wants her head scratched just so. By the time I return downstairs I have forgotten about the letters but remember I need to pay a bill so up to my office, only to decide (foolishly) I might just check email – quickly. Right. An hour later it is pushing time to feed the dogs and I haven't paid the bill or written the letters. And there are still 30 emails to answer.

Lately I've been training myself. And as long as I don't get distracted by someone or something, it works. When I find my mind and feet headed in another, off-the-cuff direction, I simply say out loud, "Rita, Halt!" And then I find myself saying rather sheepishly, "Oh, right, *that's* what I was going to do." And off I go on the project or errand initially intended. And by five in the afternoon, I feel accomplished and proud of myself.

Now, as a hopelessly creative, right-brain oriented, non-linear individual, there are exceptions to my rule that I deem to be perfectly acceptable. And I extend these here because for those of you out there who, like me, are writers, artists, musicians, poets, dancers – well, you get my point; and if you happen to also be born in the sign of Aries (a million projects going at once), and living primarily from the right hemisphere of your brain, then quite spontaneously a poem, or image, or song, or intuitive nudge will spring into our mind and well, we have to write it down right then, or it's gone. I have been known to be on my way to those infamous water buckets and see a stunning cloud formation overhead. What kind of person would I be to not turn around, go back in the house for my camera and spend twenty minutes taking multiple photographs of the cloud as it morphed into even more interesting shapes and colors? A dull, unimaginative, far too pragmatic one, I would guess. The trick is to then remember to fill the water buckets once my camera is safely stowed back inside!

Many years ago I made elaborate puppets, wrote plays for them, and performed them around the area with a friend of mine. Despite the hard work, my plays were unique, not the Punch and Judy type, but themes to inspire and delight children. Those were the gates I left open in my mind for themes and characters to arrive.

One morning as I was washing the breakfast dishes, suddenly out of absolutely nowhere relevant I saw in my mind a large blue mouse. Wearing overalls and a striped shirt. His name would be

Amos Blue. His message: It's okay to be yourself, no matter who you are or what you appear to be. I never looked back, as the saying goes.

I didn't finished the breakfast dishes until late in the afternoon, so involved was I in creating the puppet, a larger-than-life mouse made of Styrofoam, gray material with blue overlays of paint, a long sweeping tail, and huge ears and yes, overalls and a striped shirt. Long black sticks attached to the palms of his paws would move him arms. He had charisma, he had "life". Amos: A MO(u)S(e), Blue, True to himself.

Today, Amos Blue sits on my dresser watching over me, always a reminder to be glad for just who I am as my self-assessment tends to be rather condemning. And, he's a reminder to listen to my intuition inspiration and follow its gentle, positive messages.

So as I suggest to those of you who can be easily distracted, to Halt! And *try* and stick to a plan. But I would also highly recommend leaving room for the flow of inspiration. Amazing things can happen, and those necessary routines will just have to wait a bit.

Stepping up

EVERYONE HAS THEIR STRUGGLES IN life, some more intense than others, but to the individual his or her own can be as steep and daunting as the next person's. More often than not we stumble and fall but manage somehow to get ourselves back up and keep moving forward, even if at a crawl. We learn, we grow, we toughen, and perhaps we become more compassionate to others coming along behind us who need a hand up the same rock face of experience we have just traversed. We grow wiser, kinder, softer, more understanding and lenient, mellowing as judgmental creatures who used to only focus on our own needs and wants. But most of all, with each struggle and with each rebound we step further into the territory of our hearts and that aspect of our expansive soul that holds not only our humanly self, but everyone and everything as kin.

I look back on my life, impressed by the steps that have led me to right here, right now, in some kind of profound and perfect timing and perfect order, interconnected all along the way. With each step I have been nudged (and sometimes pushed) with inherent love and understanding upward on my journey to a clearer understanding of who I am – my truest *Self*. One could almost say I'm coming out of the human, ego constructed closet, emerging into the unlimited, boundless being I have been and will always be, before my birth, throughout this lifetime and after my release from the physical plane.

Those steps are not just mine, they are yours and all others as well. We share a journey through the process of life and living that cannot, at its core be differentiated by species, age, environment, or any other means of measurement. We just are; it's that simple.

Three Messages

I STOOD AT THE WINDOW in the county office building, waiting while the person on the other side of the Plexiglas processed my semi-annual property tax payment. My head was spinning with anxiety. The amount of the check I had just given her would about clean out the monthly Social Security income I had just only just received that morning. What to do?? What to do??

A small yellow card on the narrow shelf in front of me caught my eye.

Thank you
for Your Patience

it said, simple black letters against the soft background. It felt gentle and kind to me and my anxiety lifted away.

~

Earlier in the week I had to call L.L. Bean about a return. Their customer service department is always friendly and anxious to help so I was not concerned about phoning them. But as it was just before Christmas I anticipated being on hold for a while. My brain flooded with tasks waiting to be done.

The recorded message I received thanked me for contacting them and that a representative would be with me as soon as possible. But it was the next part of the recording that impressed me:

There will be silence while you wait.

And blessed silence it was, no crackly music or advertising of products, just quiet. I sighed contentedly and relaxed.

~

This morning I nearly knocked over a small metal box I keep on my bookshelf. Over the years I have collected sayings and quotes that have inspired me, writing each on a small card. I had a daily habit of randomly selecting a card, and always it would be appropriate guidance. But lately I had forgotten about the box and it had accumulated some dust. On impulse I opened the lid and pulled out a card. On it I had, some time ago, written:

Find your sacred space

~

I knew immediately what all three messages, taken together, meant. And, they were meant for me, anxious, stressed-out, impatient, always rushing, me. They were gentle reminders to be kinder to myself. As has happened since I was a child, "someone" unseen was watching over me and I guess decided a bit of a word or two to slow down and take some deep breaths was necessary. Anyway, that's what I took away from the first two messages – boiling down to two words: "Peace, Rita."

And the third message? Could also be translated to say:

You are safe; go within; peace awaits you.

Holding Earth

On my windowsill sits a small seated statue of Kwan Yin. Her face, the epitome of serenity, looks down to her lap where her folded hands hold a tiny sphere of the same clay-like material from which she is made. She is, in Mahayana Buddhism, the bodhisattva of compassion and mercy and her name is often translated to mean "She who hears the cries of the world." The sphere she holds in her hands is the world.

Our Earth, the sum total of it, from oceans to mountains, elephants to microbes, ticks to giraffes and the entire scope of humanity. This goddess of compassion holds us all equally with utmost care and tends to Life as it infuses every aspect and being of our planetary home.

I pass by my little statue every day when I open or close curtains, lift or shut the window behind her, and trim and water the many plants and trees that share the room with her. There is life and light flowing through and around her, and when the afternoon sun comes around, she is illuminated.

How easily I can turn toward the shadow side of my mind and become consumed with fear, distress, frustration, sometimes even anger, although not so much of that anymore. Still, I can feel my blood pressure rise, my pulse speed up, and my breathing begin to tighten. The walls of my emotions close in, constricting me in every way.

But there sits Kwan Yin, reminding me that I, too, am held in her tenderness. I remember that just as she does, I love all of Earth and her beings and also feel empathy for those who suffer the sadness and pain that can descend so swiftly and cut so deep. There before me on my windowsill and in my heart is the Goddess of mercy and compassion, holding us close, her large Spirit Self embracing us in her cupped hands, the energy of her love flowing through us all without condition.

So in my despairing moments I stop, fold my hands together as if in my lap, and imagine the whole world as a tiny, perfect sphere resting there. And I know I am not alone, for as I feel the presence of my beloved Kwan Yin before me, sadness leaves me and peace once again, returns.

Remembering Adventure

First snow of the season fell overnight and into today, transforming the landscape and stirring those diehard joyous memories of growing up in Connecticut where the snows were deep, frequent, and magical. In those days, I built snowmen and igloos from the towering piles shoveled high onto the sides of our long driveway by diligent adults It was all Adventure.

This morning, over six decades later, I went right to work way before dawn, warming the donkeys' water tank, cleaning out their barn, and giving them grain and hay. Then out to the front of the house to fill bird feeders, clear snow, and hang out fresh suet.

Still dark out and snowing heavily, I returned to the dogs' garden to clear various paths for two of my three old dogs. While Snowy at 13 is fine with it all, Lillie, my 10-year old with anxieties about stepping on different textures of ground, can become catatonic if she senses something cold and/or wet under her paws. So returning her usual path to dirt level is essential. Jonathan, ancient miniature poodle (he's pushing 18), always ploughs on through the snow, but this morning became disoriented when I let him out, missed his usual path, and ended up stuck in a drift. Totally blind now, he uses his sense of smell to guide him, but the snow had masked those familiar "guideposts". He was quickly rescued and carried back to the warm house and a biscuit for comfort.

Those essential steps taken, my responsible grownup-self stepped back outside to turn my face to the descending snow-flakes, letting my childhood, New England delight rebound throughout my senses and relax into the mesmerizing silence only snow can bring.

As daylight began to crest the eastern mountains across the road, the first of the small birds, white-throated and English sparrows, chickadees, juncos and nuthatches barely visible in the dim light began to descend on the feeders and suet, the delicate sound of their wings stirring the quiet. A first visiting squirrel chattered close by, and the long, deeper wing-beats of blue jays, cardinals and crows added depth to the morning symphony as I stood still so as to not disturb them. Then I slowly eased back inside to join the dogs in the warmth of the living room.

The day would now unfurl into critter feeding, breakfast, and the usual morning chores. Undoubtedly the phone would ring, cars and trucks would move slowly down the snow-packed road, ploughs and salt trucks would rumble along, and my mind would turn, with a large sigh, to the huge pile of paperwork waiting for me in my office.

But magic never really disappears into that which we consider reality – the five-senses world of grown-up responsibilities, obligations, schedules, and that infamous To Do list that looms before most of us.

For always at the ready are those delights that come by many names to enchant us, give us even a brief holiday from the world we trudge through. And these delights may be wonderful child-hood memories, or discoveries made as adults, such as the overwhelming sense of companionship and love that comes with caring for animals, especially (for me) the closeness of the old and special-needs ones. The soft warm breath on my face of my donkeys in the earliest hours of morning, the eagerness of my dogs as they wait for their first treats, the purring, welcoming response of my cats as I bring them their food, the gathering of birds and squirrels at the feeders, deer standing keen-eyed at the edge of my little forest. These are beyond abundance in my consideration, gifts without cost or need of repayment – the purity of reciprocity without compensation or contingency.

Soon winter will pass away taking its snows with it, and spring will step forward. I won't be shoveling paths for the dogs or clearing ice from water buckets, but the early memories of *spring* in Connecticut will emerge: bird nests high in the Horse Chestnut tree, first leaves on the old elm tree, out in back of the barn, iris and daffodils unfurling in my grandmother's garden. And they will blend into my own Virginia spring as that deep blue peace of the pre-dawn mountains begins my day. Lillie will be happy to have dirt beneath her paws again, and Jonathan, old soul, if he is still with me will take his time following familiar scents while Snowy, my constant companion, will pad along beside me.

Two of a Kind

A BRILLIANTLY SUNNY, BREEZY SPRING day and I was hanging laundry on the clothesline. I reached into the plastic bucket in which I keep my wooden clothespins. I had just added some new ones – their smooth, fresh wood and easy spring were pleasant to work with. But the next one my hand picked up had been around a long time, rough to the touch, a bit crooked, the wood stained and chipped. When I tried to squeeze the ends, the spring hung back and I could hardly open it. Arthritis in both my hands requires ease of operating anything, especially something as small as a clothespin. This was just too difficult.

I set the old clothespin to the side to toss away later. It was useless to me. But my hand had hardly set it down when again, intuitively, I reached for it. I turned it over and over in my own stiff fingers, and suddenly I saw it so differently! No longer was it a machine-fashioned clothespin, but an old friend who had seen kinder days health-wise, a smoother, unblemished exterior, and a fluid joint. I studied it carefully. The spring was, yes, a bit bent, but still intact, still ready to serve its purpose, but would need a bit more help. The wood, somewhat pitted and gouged from years of use, reminded me of a very old, antique table I had once wanted to buy and add to my household. And I realized two things. First of all, I was, in effect, looking at myself, a bit stiff and certainly not so young anymore, but with some help I could certainly still do my job. Did I want to be judged as otherwise and tossed aside, rejected for who I am now?

And secondly, I felt real love for this old helper of mine. Holding the aged pin in the palm of my hand, I felt such companionship with it – is that silly? Hardly. After all, we are just two of a kind.

I gently placed the weathered clothespin in my pocket – certainly it deserved respect – and to retire, it had served well, with nobility and dedication, holding up clothes on the line so they might dry in the sun and breeze.

Now it sits propped up on my kitchen windowsill where I continue to respect and admire it and we share stories about getting old.

The Welcome Chair

THERE IS A CHAIR IN my living room that has both presence and personality. It has shared its life in two homes that I know of, the first being that of a dear English friend, and now my own. Further history remains the chair's secret.

It's not a fancy chair, nor does it have multiple functions such as a recliner would. It does not rock, but is steadfast on its four beautifully carved, dark wooden legs. To many people accustomed to more formal or ornate furniture, this one would quite likely appear plain and uninteresting. Yet it is, in its simplicity of line, graceful by design and gracious by character. And to me it is very beautiful – for three reasons.

To look upon this chair is pleasing to the eye. The arms are of narrow, gently curved wood, smooth to the touch, offering the image of an open, inviting embrace. With a favorite book in hand and time to spare, one would find it difficult to resist its call.

Across the white and softly padded seat and back drapes a multi-colored afghan of mellow green, blue, and maroon, reminiscent of a piece of finely woven tapestry fabric from the Twelfth Century – perhaps French or Italian, adding an air of ancestral wisdom.

To settle into the chair is pleasing to the soul, holding its visitor in a companionable way. A sense of comradery between human and chair grows until it is quite possible (and has often been reported as so) that the spirit of this otherwise unassuming piece of furniture and the spirit of its guest begin to blend in a most endearing way.

Many beings other than humans are also respectfully held here: Snowy, my elderly dog companion takes turns with Emma-Anne, resident wildling feline. Sunlight settles across it in late afternoons; soft lamplight in the evening.

Light-streams of another kind – contemplation, meditation, and day-dreaming – are encouraged, allowing oneself to be adrift in space/time within the safety of a vessel so sturdy, comfortable, and dependable.

And lastly, inspiration flows easily to those who sit here with a quiet mind, as if this chair is a gateway to an unseen realm, a transporter of Mind to magical places, fanciful, or perhaps truly real after all. (After all, it was within this chair I was inspired to write about it.)

If you were to visit and your heart is open, you will quite likely feel this remarkable chair silently, humbly say to you:

Welcome, friend!
Come, rest yourself awhile.

Necessary

THE GARDEN POND NEEDS FILLING; it didn't rain enough last night. Now the bird bath wants cleaning. Do the crows have to walk in it?

Oh, oh – grass is growing in the stone path again, but tiniest blue flowers, too. I just can't pull them....

I should sweep the porch. It's only mid-August, but leaves are falling on it, all over the chairs and table; what if company drops by? What would they think?

The male cardinal calls to me from the cedar tree. I should fill the feeders. But looking upward to his brilliance among green boughs, now I see the mountains: Sun and cloud skim across their broad, soft sides, a hawk rides the air currents unencumbered by the endless tasks we humans feel are so necessary.

I *should* keep working, not just stand here. But for just a while I will stop, be silent, really look at everything and pay attention to every sound, color, shape, and shadow, everything and everyone perfect as they are.

And to realize that is all that is, right now, necessary.

EWC

When I was a small child living in Texas, my father had two nicknames for me. One was Dennis the Menace after the cartoon boy who, with a slingshot in the back pocket of his overalls, was always in trouble. His other name for me was "Don't-Fence-Me-In-Rita" after a popular cowboy song of the time. And my mother's name for me was her Wild Little Irish, pretty much summing up my emerging personality from birth to age four.

The following year my father disappeared from my life so I have no idea how he would have continued to view his growing daughter. But my mother's opinion was clear: I was always the renegade of the family, moving at breakneck speed in every direction, wanting to learn, to see, to know everything simultaneously. I let little stop me. Naturally, with such bravado I was often in trouble, hardly ever played by the rules, and never, ever, liked being told what to do by those adults who felt they knew what was best for me. Once my exhausted mother said to me, "Rita Carol, I don't know where you came from. You are *so bad*, you could not have come from me." Harsh words for a child to hear, even though in fairness to her I must have been a handful.

My parents divorced when I was five and my mother, sister, Sylvia, and I moved to Connecticut to live with my grandmother;

in her I found my first soulmate. Elizabeth (Elsie) Williams Chandler, or EWC as she preferred to be called, was as much a renegade as I and often in just as much trouble with her daughter, my mother. Mom's nickname for Elsie was, not surprising, "My Wild Little Mother."

But that same boundless philosophy and her wild and determined spirit had saved Elsie repeatedly during extremely difficult times and while diminutive in size – barely four foot eleven – her spunk and recklessness kept her on her feet, refusing defeat. Because I was in admiring awe of her, the core of my grandmother's survival tactics she passed along to me, her "partner in crime," tactics and practices that have likewise served me so well.

I wonder if she saw much of herself in me and while each of our personal stories were of different historical times, from early childhood on we would reflect each other on so many levels. As a young child she, too, lost a vital part of her family when she and her brother Morrie were adopted by a doctor and his wife. As the story I was told goes, their parents, very young themselves, were too poor to support them.

But most of the stories I have heard regarding my Granny's life involved her husband Henry Williams Chandler, my grandfather. He was a brilliant man, professor of economics, and master of the financial world with a keen eye for fine art and literature. But as a husband and father he fell far short, inflicting extreme control over, and pain and suffering on his wife and three daughters. My mother, as the eldest, bore the brunt of his temper and abuse. My grandmother did what she could to protect herself and her children and her stubbornly strong spirit drove her to stand firm in creative ways against her husband.

Elsie's life must have had its frightening, even terrifying and demoralizing times. Even so her courage, faith, determination to survive, and her intense love of life carried her forward. She was a poet, writer, gardener, artist, and humanitarian. Decades ahead of the times, she never hesitated to take care of others no matter their age, color or religion. If a person was sick or a family was lacking adequate food or clothes, she was at their door offering help, friendship and support. In her community and far beyond she was both loved and respected without exception. And I adored her.

My grandmother was the one person in my immediate family who understood my independent soul – that which I was born with – and the aching desire to explore and expand the boundaries, to break the rules set by my mother and be, completely, who I wanted and needed to be. Along the way Granny inspired the innate writer in me and taught me the art of both appreciating and writing poetry. She encouraged my imagination and its importance in following a life of creativity. She taught me about angels and validated for me my first experience with my own guardian angel. Early in her life she had set her path and forged ahead; she encouraged me to do the same: to love beauty, to be generous and grateful, to look around corners for the unexpected and unexplained and revel in their mystery, and to never let anyone tell me what they thought I should be. And when I fell down, as I would inevitably do, she told me to pick myself up, tend to the scraped knees of my spirit and forge on, always keeping the light and love that shines within every being, clear and in my sights.

I am still that same Wild Little Irish – insatiably inquisitive and independent – who so frustrated my mother, but delighted my Granny. While my admittedly aging body slows me down, I still want to discover, do and be absolutely everything possible. Before I could define it, instinctively I knew my life on this planet was an incredible gift, not to be taken lightly or for granted.

There are advantages and disadvantages to every age we experience. There are things now I am no longer able to physically do, and realize I never will again this time around. But my passion remains intact and alert. I still get up at 5:00 in the morning to be out in the barn to my donkeys before first light. They are, after all, my dear friends. I have to be out of bed to hear the Whip-Poor-Will in summer, and in winter to see the stars high and around me in the cold, clear sky. I will stand awestruck by the Milky Way overhead in June and the Andromeda Galaxy in December. And I am determined that always there will be at least some small part of me who is Dennis the Menace, refusing to be fenced in.

I was fifteen when my grandmother died and I felt my life fall apart on so many levels. In my free fall I declared to myself that I would live – and die – the way she had. In her mid-Seventies, she suffered a major heart attack. In those days (the 1950s) a cardiac patient was given bed rest for six weeks and my grandmother was given her orders. Though frustrated, she did comply. But in her undaunted and spirited manner she sat up in her bed week after week, learning to read and write the Greek language. Then at some point after her recovery she moved herself from the house in Connecticut to her own apartment in Arizona, to live her life according to her choosing, overflowing with delight, as it turns out to have been.

Two days before her 80th birthday, she opened the birthday box we had sent to her. Then she attended her yoga class, went on to her Japanese brush painting class, then drove out into the desert to do a water color painting of the land she loved so well. Later than night she called her doctor and her closest friends to tell them that she was having another heart attack, thanked them for their friendship, wished them all well, and died. Mystic that she was, three days earlier she had written in pencil on a scrap of paper the following words:

I break with the past and keep what I've learned for my new walking.

Even though I know she continues to watch over me, I will always miss her.

I am, of course, myself. I loudly declared that when I was born, so I'm told. And I am, proudly, Elsie's granddaughter. Following in her footsteps, I live my life according to the teachings that she embodied, keeping my senses alive for new understanding of being and living in more profound, kind and wise ways.

Islands
(More about Elsie)

WHAT A BIG OCEAN IS this life! Tumbling or calm, deep and dark green or tropical turquoise blue; giant, thunderous waves of circumstance crashing over our little boat of days, or placid, soothing swells that smooth our passage. We hardly know what to expect across the horizon: jagged rocks? Soft white sandy beach? How do we set our sails when the wind keeps changing direction, when cloudless skies turn suddenly black? How best to make it from shore to shore, from birth into this life to birth into the next?

My grandmother's method was to create what she called "Islands", places and means of refuge when the storms raged, catching her up in their torrents and winds. And for her such islands were her poetry, her three daughters, the gardens, her watercolor painting, and her friends. Throughout those tumultuous times that would seem to engulf her, she moved with courage and grace from island to island, always keeping her head above water – maybe sometimes just, but enough to set her sights on the next place of rest and rejuvenation.

Few people I have known have had a life free of obstacles and storms. "Never been a sick a day in my life;" "Always have plenty of money;" "Isn't it all just so perfect?" "Chronic pain? What's that?" Wouldn't all of that be wonderful! Forget that challenges make us stronger and poverty makes us grateful. *Really?* Not for me, thank you. I've had my share of being tossed about on that vast ocean, this little boat now creaking and a bit lower in the water of existence. But still sailing! And, still adopting my grandmother's survival technique of building islands as I go and staying above the waterline – maybe, admittedly, sometimes just – when the changeable seas of life get rough.

My islands are just that, my own and I encourage everyone to look for those in their own life, perhaps something as tiny as a beautiful flower growing in the lawn or a favorite book or piece of music. It could be time with a really good friend; an afternoon on the front porch; the unrivaled companionship of a cat, dog, horse, donkey, bird, or any other creature; listening to frogs sing at night, or crickets in fall. The possibilities are right at hand and waiting for all of us who seek them.

Franny

DESPITE THE CHALLENGES WE GAVE each other, my mother, Francis Chandler Morris, or Franny as she preferred to be called, was the key person in my childhood to recognize in me a deep love for and connection with everything in nature. I may have caused her endless anxiety and frustration, but she never discouraged the habit I had of bringing home all manner of creatures in my pockets, or playing "Indian" – (never cowboys for whom I had only disdain) and all that was entailed: covering my arms, legs and face with red brick dust, respecting every tiny bug or leaf with utmost concern and care, exclaiming the wind was my friend and rocks were alive, beings in their own right. I wanted moccasins for footwear and she found me a kit in a craft store so that I could make my own. She helped me fashion a bow from a stick and string, advising me to imagine the arrows! And she read to me about our Native Peoples and how they were the first true custodians of our land.

So while my grandmother Elsie encouraged my creativity, adventurous impulses, and angelic encounters, my mother encouraged my innate mystical tendencies and my stubborn, unshakeable belief that all life is sacred, even down to my enormous collection of stuffed animals all of whom I just knew were alive in their own way.

When I was about eight years old, my grandmother gave me my first large picture book about Albert Schweitzer with stunning black and white photos of the great man with his animals. The book was aptly entitled, *The Animal World of Albert Schweitzer.* Bingo! I was hooked and all these decades later Dr. Schweitzer remains my greatest mentor and inspiration. In later years my mother added to my Schweitzer collection with various other volumes not only about him, but his own personal writings on religion, music, and mysticism.

Franny, or Mommy as my sister and I lovingly called her, was, herself, a shattered soul, having suffered enormous abuse by her father when she was a child and young adult, and then at the hands of *my* father. Still, she carried that strong gene passed down from her mother, my grandmother, which has been passed in turn to both my sister and myself. She was, in a word, a survivor.

We certainly had our issues – mother/daughter stuff not uncommon in families. My mother often found my wild, adventurous spirit difficult to control, and as a dedicated parent – and a single parent at that – I am sure she often despaired over how this determined child would turn out. But despite our differences we shared that deep, immovable honor for those of the forest, fields, mountains, desert, ocean and meadow. Even when most at odds with each other, in that common ground we deeply loved, understood, and respected one another.

As we both grew older and I, for one, began to mature, we shared more and more of our inner thoughts and mystical tendencies. I was no longer that strange creature called Teenager who was embarrassed when my mother refused to dye her graying hair, or allowed her front lawn to become enlightened with dandelions and little oak seedlings in a neighborhood of manicured lawns.

My mother, as always, remained true to what she believed in – kindness, gentleness, and respect for others. And while it took some years of experiencing and hard consideration on my part, I came to align with her in every way.

Always an artist, adventurer, writer, and mystic at heart, Franny joined my grandmother in being among the finest teachers and caregivers I could have ever chosen for myself. My mother who longed to be a gypsy, my grandmother who knew the angels: two remarkable, strong, vibrant women who brought me to where I am today.

"Where Only Chaos Shows...."

THIS IS THE FINAL LINE in the poem, *Assurance*,* written in the mid- 1900s by my grandmother, Elsie. It is a poem that always anchors me when the turbulence of crisis seems to toss me about as if beyond my will or my control. And I add the words "seems to" because here is the rest of her poem:

Assurance
One's strength is greater than one knows:
Hard pressed,
It bridges chasms dark with doubt
And gropes through daunting mists
With powers of faith unguessed
To hold a path
Where only chaos shows.

"through daunting mists...." Recently, because of longterm Lyme Disease my body ambushed me. First my knee blew out, then my legs, then my back and left hip and finally my elbow, as if all of me was tumbling like dominoes once stacked neatly, now falling in rapid succession, pushing one another down. Walking became hobbling, holding onto walls and doorways, fences and

stair rails, whatever was at hand. Standing, sitting, lying down all caused pain of enormous proportions – there was no clear cause, no obvious remedy. I leaned heavily into the harsh reality of how fragile we can be.

My busy life of rushing here and there slowed to near stand-still, only the very necessary tasks were tended to. Most of the people (outside my own family of two and four-footeds), out of necessity were set aside while I focused all my remaining energy on myself and those immediately close to me.

I became frightened. Can I say it aloud? Terrified. I, who had always successfully overcome every obstacle through perseverance and hard work, I who came from that long line of survivors, I who had met and won over every challenge for decades, felt impending defeat. Who would take care of my animals? Where would this strange condition take me, these "chasms dark with doubt?"

"hard pressed...." Decidedly so. Six AM, my usual first rounds outside, I toddled like a small child across the yard from house to barn, using my outstretched arms to balance me against the pain coursing across my lower back and down my legs. *Nope, not going to give up or give in....pain meds should be kicking in soon.* My beloved cow watched me unconcerned. I would emerge from the feed room with fresh hay for her, this she knew, even if *I* wondered how. Her confidence in me pushed me on; how could I disappoint her? From the opposite fence my two donkeys called softly to me. A longer stretch of yard to cover, but I could do it: *scoop up the hay, find my footing, walk along leaning against the outer wall of the barn... to the gate. Almost there. Now to clean stalls, push the wheelbarrow, empty it at the far end of the fence line.*

Ever so painful and slow but see! not impossible. Step by step, pay attention, I can do it.

And with hay finally delivered, stalls cleaned, manure dumped and gates closed behind me, usually all small easy tasks done effortlessly. I felt strong in my spirit if not my body, even though it had taken me more than twice as long. "Look to the bright side," my grandmother used to tell me.

So indeed, *"One's strength is greater than one knows...."* I eased over to my cow, kissed the topknot of white hair between her ears, and scratched her under the chin, then rested against her soft, russet body. When I again straightened up pain shot through my hips and I stumbled forward grasping onto her vast neck for support. Sensing my distress, she leaned gently into me as if to hold me, body and soul, and licked my hand. The pain bowed away before such love. I felt invincible!

To hold a path.... I worked my way with more confidence now toward the kitchen door. I realized how grateful I had become for every step accomplished and I anticipated not agony and struggle, but breakfast as I moved forward, steady and strong in the comforting reality of how very resilient we truly are.

*from *Of Roots I Sing, *by Elsie Williams Chandler, 1958.*

Helen

When I was 20 the world and my life was calm and uneventful. I had had a few "bumps" in my life up until then, such as losing my father when I was five, but my health was good and I lacked for little.

At the time, I was employed at the Concord Bookshop in Concord, MA and counted among my friends and fellow workers a lovely, gracious older woman named Helen. I would have guessed her to be in her late 60s, a widow who lived alone in the small gatehouse of a local estate. We often discussed literature, as by then I was an avid reader and writer. Helen – tall, elegant, and gracious – was soft-spoken and kind, always encouraging me in my writing endeavors.

One day she did not come to work and I learned that the evening before, on her way to dinner with friends, she had developed an embolism in her spine. Now paralyzed from the waist down, she was not expected to ever walk again.

In time she returned to her little home with live-in help. She was, understandably, discouraged but, I was told, also determined to eventually walk again and live independently, despite the seemingly impossible odds.

Some weeks later I visited her. As I opened the front door

there she was, standing tall, walking towards me! She had two canes for support, carefully pushing her feet forward, a miracle no one thought would ever happen.

But Helen, from the start, knew differently. As gently and consistently as she had encouraged me in my personal life, so had she done the same for herself, never once turning away from the possibility of once again being mobile, or allowing herself to descend into self-pity and hopelessness. But she also had a beacon to follow: her spirit, ever strong, always saw the ultimate best in everyone and everything no matter how dire the situation and in this belief, she held her faith. "Everything always eventually works out for the best," she would remind me and those words and her courage have been *my* beacon and strength on many occasions over the years.

Untangling Knots in the Ribbon of Life

SOMETIMES — OKAY, INEVITABLY, THE ribbon of life that we follow knots up. Because I do have that forward-rush-think-it-through-later habit, this happens quite often for me. The day is going along fine, then suddenly it lurches, doubles back on itself and tangles into an ungodly knot. Confusion follows, and that "Oh-oh" moment of realization that I messed up. It's really no use to mope around in regret or guilt — but a knot begs to be untangled, the ribbon straightened, and life to once again return to Smooth. After all, it *is* difficult to find one's balance and center point of peace in a knotty situation.

Some years ago I was in my local Super Wal-Mart. Not the happiest time of my life, I was completely exhausted physically, mentally, and emotionally. To add to my current misery, mindlessly loading up my grocery cart with items that were not that appealing only darkened my mood.

A voice spoke to me at my elbow. "Excuse me," someone said softly and politely.

I looked down and there beside me was a man in a wheelchair. His face reflected my mood, but little was getting past my own wall of unhappiness.

"Could you please tell where I would find paper towels?" the man asked. He looked so defeated, but my own sense of defeat apparently closed down my usual tendency to rush into rescue mode.

"Of course," I replied. "Right around the next aisle – by the bath tissue and napkins." He thanked me and wheeled himself around the corner and out of sight. I pushed my cart in the opposite direction, continuing with my shopping.

But something was very wrong. All my insides were beginning to knot up. My brain was starting to hurt, I thought I felt my heart give a small whimper. By the time I figured out the knot in this scenario, I was four aisles over in canned soup.

Good grief, what had I been thinking? *That fellow, down in his wheelchair, could not possibly reach the shelves of paper towels! Why had I not gone with him and retrieved for him what he needed?* I rushed back to find him, but he was gone – I had not passed him, and even with further searching came up empty and my knot just got tighter and tighter.

I apologized to Whomever might be listening, vowed to do better next time, and let it go. What more could I do? But this particular knot in the ribbon of my life hung in with determination.

Two weeks later I was in another grocery store, deep in the shelves of the natural foods section. A woman, no one I knew, perhaps ten years my senior and an inch shorter than I, eased toward me, her eyes scanning the shelves. I heard a distinct sigh of frustration. Ah ha!!! I sprang into action, being careful to not knock her over in my enthusiasm. I was so glad to see her, this stranger in distress. I asked her if I could help her find something.

"Oh," she replied with familiar weariness. "I can't find the organic applesauce and I've been up and down these shelves so many times."

I pointed to a high shelf and cheerily said, "Let me get it for you!" Jar of organic applesauce collected and carefully given into her possession, I smiled at her, my gratitude profound. Had my heart begged for another chance to set things straight regarding my previous lack of good judgment? Apples (sauce) to paper goods, what mattered was that I had, finally, paid attention and my rescue mode was back in full gear.

I felt the knot untangle, the ribbon smooth, and the day and I went forward.

I can only hope some kind soul helped the fellow obtain his paper towels. I also wondered if he were not more of a lesson offered me that I, well, didn't do so great on. But the universe is forgiving, I got to take the test again, and I think I passed. In all the times since I have been in Wal-Mart I have never again seen the man in the wheelchair. But I will never stop thanking him for reminding me to pay attention to the call of my heart and do the right thing.

Cookies Before Soup...
Or how to play with convention

CLEMENT CAMPBELL WAS A GOOD friend of my grandmother Elsie when we lived in Connecticut. Quite often he would venture from his apartment in New York City to share Sunday lunch with us, always an exciting time for me when family and close friends gathered. I remember him coming up the walk to the front door wearing his long gray overcoat – I don't recall much else about him as I was only about 7 or 8 at the time. He did have great, thick magical fingers that would play Bach on our old upright piano, the music permeating the entire house. "Uncle" Clement (a relative in name only) was the organist for Saint Patrick's Cathedral in New York, and not until our mother took my sister and me to visit it, did I understand the enormity of his profession and fame.

To me he was just Uncle Clement, a quiet but witty man with sparkling eyes and always a funny story to share. A brilliant musician with a seriously impressive intellect, he made me feel appreciated and special. Seeing me for the creative, expressive (and often frustrated as a result) child that I was, I was secure knowing that he truly supported and encouraged me, despite my being "Dennis the Menace" to certain other members of my family!

One such Sunday luncheon I stood by Uncle Clement at the dining room table as my grandmother prepared the meal in the kitchen and he sliced and buttered the warm, freshly baked bread. At barely four feet tall, I peeked over the top of the great oak table, watching him intently. He turned and looked down at me and in all seriousness calmly said, "Would you like butter on one side, or two?" There was that infamous twinkle in his eyes he could not suppress, and you know what I replied. I've been in love with fresh bread and butter ever since.

Sometimes playing with convention is a good thing – it helps us see things with a different perspective, a door swinging wide to new adventure beyond. Who would think warm bread buttered on *both* sides could be so delicious! Oh what my beloved Uncle Clement unleashed in this wild Irish child! Consider warm chocolate chip cookies swerved before the healthy vegetable soup. Or opening windows in December to let in fresh air, even if the temperature outside is 48 degrees. What about, just once in a while, skipping doing the laundry to sit in the garden? Or buying that irresistible book and *then* paying the utility bill?

There are many ways to set convention aside and dare to try something new or different, to just not be sensible for once, not even be a grownup, but if only briefly be that child again that always did things her own way. And yes, usually got in trouble for it, but also secretly knew it was more than worth it.

Uncle Clement hovers over me, I have no doubt, though he's been gone from this life for nearly 50 years. And my grandmother Elsie: the supreme teacher of convention-busting, my best pal for so many years, I often feel her close. No wonder she and Clement Campbell were such devoted friends. With them around in spirit how could I possibly be anything but the adventurous self I am today?

The first quarter of the Twenty-first Century is plagued by war and terrorism, frightening politics, a health care system run amok, and violence and greed around most corners. But not all, because around some corners of life are really good friends, the Uncle Clements and Elsie Williams Chandlers, Bach played on an old upright piano, and fresh bread right out of the oven. So have a chocolate chip cookie – the soup can wait a bit, it's time to step aside from the rules and have an adventure.

Author's note: The inspiration for this chapter came after a dream I had recently in which Uncle Clement, in his old gray overcoat, was coming up the walkway to the old Connecticut house. He came straight toward me, my all grown-up self, and with utmost affection in his eyes, smiled at me. And the dream ended. I awoke knowing he was checking on me to make sure I was all right, or maybe to see if I was still willing to butter my bread on both sides. And the answer is a resounding Yes!

Teachers and Friends
of Other Realms

THE FOLLOWING PAGES OFFER JUST a few of the many experiences and thoughts offered to me for over most of my life beginning in early childhood. The thoughts and images have come not audibly or visually, but in signs and impressions, some in profound dreams that stay with me in perfect clarity years after they have occurred; some through the creatures who have shared my home and heart; and some from realms or worlds of higher vibration than ours, those of the angels and spirit guides.

Everything shared with me from any of these sources has always been deep, timeless wisdom, direction, and unconditional, supreme love of the most embracing yet allowing kind. How to describe all of this adequately with words? Extremely difficult, for when one is privy to such realms, what may make sense on a time/space linear manner, becomes fluid and unbounded and incredibly awesome. But also difficult to put into words on a page. But I will try!

I make no claims to being special, gifted, or spiritually advanced, just open minded and willing to accept the extraordinary.

My Tibetan Lama

TOBE SPOKE TO ME BEFORE I even saw him.

July 2001. I knew there was another dog coming here. I could feel the pull in my bones, familiar after 23 years of tending to homeless animals. Trusting my intuition, I went to the local shelter, walked the cages, looked in all those eyes, but the dog I felt coming closer, calling to me all the time now, was not there. I left empty-handed and confused.

The next day the summer newsletter from the Caring for Creatures Animal Sanctuary in Fluvanna County, Virginia arrived in my mailbox. Inside was a picture and description of Leo, a mid-sized, elderly terrier who needed a home. Instantly, I knew he was the one I had been sensing.

Two weeks later on August First Leo came to be with our family. Thought by the original examining veterinarian to be nine years old, to me he seemed much older, or else his life had been exceptionally hard. "Found by Greene County couple in early February '01," the adoption papers said, "emaciated, weak, and disoriented...nursed back to health and brought to Caring For Creatures." Furthermore, the veterinarian's analysis of Leo's mental and physical condition was daunting:

"Lays around all night; circles a lot to the left; raspy breathing. Not relating to humans. Is emaciated, barely able to walk. Doesn't hear very well. Circles and paces, able to walk straight if prompted. Obsessive- compulsive…"

Leo, I was told, seemed to live in a world of his own, but he was gentle and quiet – no one at the Sanctuary had heard him bark. He settled in contentedly his first night here, as if sure of where he was despite the intense interest of the other dogs and variety of cats,. Without a fuss, he curled into a tight ball on the new bed I had made for him and went to sleep.

I liked the name given him at the Sanctuary, considering he had arrived here under the astrological sign of Leo, and his coat was tawny and thick like a lion's. But sometime in that first night I sat up straight, drawn sharply from deep sleep. I heard myself saying the word "Tobe" – and clearly, it was spelled in that manner, rather than *Toby*. Simultaneously, with absolute certainty I knew two things: Leo's name was actually, or should be, *Tobe*, and the name implied *To Be*. And - Tobe was not just another old, homeless, starving dog to be rescued. He had chosen to come to me as my teacher and guide, to remind me To Just Be, a lesson I have needed all my life.

From then on I called him Tobe, and while Mary Birkholz (Founder and Director of Caring For Creatures) said he had never responded to "Leo," he definitely turned or raised his head when I used his new name. One day a year later, I called out to the Sanctuary about another animal and talked with Cheryl, one of the office workers. "How is Leo?" she asked.

"He's fine," I replied, "but you know, I changed his name to Tobe shortly after he came here."

There was a long silence. "Oh," Cheryl finally said. "You

know, when he first came to the Sanctuary, I thought *he looks more like a Tobe.*"

My own veterinarian gave Tobe a thorough examination, putting his age, then, in 2001 at around 14 or 15. This made more sense because of his physical appearance and problems. His persistent circling to the left was most likely due to an old (now absent) inner ear infection that had caused permanent damage. He was, indeed, mostly deaf and completely blind from Progressive Retinal Atrophy, a condition common to terriers. The muscles in his back legs were atrophied from age, making rising and lying down on his own difficult and painful. Toward the end of the first year with me, he could only walk if I held onto his tail. I was beginning to wonder if it would be kinder to release him from his tired, very old body.

Not so, my intuition told me firmly. It occurred to me that I might strengthen those back muscles if we walked up and down the sloped, short driveway several times each day. Then we'd walk around one of the smaller pastures near the barn, he being silent while I chatted away. He apparently had nothing to say, but so much to communicate, for when I, too, would become silent on our walking trips, often strange and wise thoughts would come into my head, all relative to the difficult (for me) process of learning To Just Be. My favorite was a poem of sorts, now my mantra, and in my mind I saw it written out as follows:

How we live our lives

Is what survives,

And love

Above

All.

I remember stopping and just staring at him – there was no doubt he was sending the words to me. Who was this dog, anyway?

Then one day I noticed that Tobe seemed to be doing fine without my holding onto his tail. Sure enough, he was chugging along on his own, his legs much stronger, his stride long and steady. And the wisdom continued to pour through my mind.

My silent terrier friend with the bright, knowing eyes: I called him my Tibetan lama, because despite all his physical difficulties he was always so steady and calm, looking straight into and through me, seeing me in completeness, accepting me without judgment. And though he spent the greater part of his days and nights sleeping, when he was awake he was fully present and attentive. And relating well, at least to this human, his student.

Old in dog years (at least 16) Tobe began to cross through that barrier called "age" as he became ageless, his ancient soul-self emerging more each day while physically his health began to slowly fade. Still eating well and content during the day, his nights were difficult and restless. Senility was taking its toll. As I had done so often in the past with other animals in my care, I began to watch closely for signs that Tobe was ready to move on. And, of course, we had that famous talk that I have with all my animals when they are preparing to die, that it was okay for him to leave.

One evening I was sitting on the floor with him, telling him about letting go, and he put his head in my lap. I closed my eyes and something happened I can hardly define in words. We both seemed to just be light – no bodies, only souls – perfectly blended. All borders between us dissolved and we were floating as one being. Intuitively I knew that we had always been this way – it felt so familiar – and we always would be so. Only for our brief time on the physical plane had we taken on material bodies that made us appear separate. Our souls would always be undivided. I had finally experienced what it was truly like to Just Be.

Early the next morning, following another difficult night for Tobe, I worried that he might now be suffering. As is my practice I asked for guidance from my own spirit helpers on knowing when to help him on, when *he* was ready, and of course, I asked him as well. Then I rose from where I was sitting beside him and went into the bedroom to make the bed. There, right in the middle of the dark purple blanket lay a small, soft white feather, almost like a down feather and I knew without question that it was the answer I had asked for. Tobe was ready to be helped on. The feather? Where had it come from? All the windows were closed and I had no birds in the house. It had to be sent by "angelic" means. For whenever I bury a creature I always place a white feather under their paw or wing for them to "fly Home on."

Later that day my ancient Tibetan Lama made his leap into Light with the kind help of my veterinarian. I have never regretted my decision to help him on.

Photons of the Soul
(More about Light)

I, AS MY SOUL, AM the connecting thread that weaves together this story. I am supported in the tapestry I have been creating, by the natural world, my human friends and family, various objects, and by angels, guides, and companions of spirit and light. Together we have traveled this life, perhaps many before this one and many more to come. We are a team with the goal of encouraging a reverence for life itself through the continual expression of unbounded love.

But what is "soul" and how do we find ours? Mystics through the ages have tried to discover and define soul, some have come up with rather convincing definitions. But I believe soul is a personal thing, like a fingerprint, unique to each being whether human, animal, bird, insect, plant, tree, landform, Earth herself... who is to say all of these do *not* have a soul? If we can't adequately define what soul is, how can we say who does and does not have one? As an artist creates a painting, does she then give it a soul, a form of life of its own? Does this book contain a soul, become a kind of living entity? What about music, or a table? Interesting ideas to ponder – but we can't prove, nor dis-prove any of it. Or can we?

Years ago, while crossing the back lawn to hang out laundry, I was suddenly aware of myself as my soul – I can't fully explain what it felt like, or why it happened, I just felt different, lighter, no longer confined to my physical body. I knew I was my soul with the same assurance as I knew I was still walking, holding my laundry basket. The sensation lasted maybe 15 seconds, but it was enough to get my attention. I do remember not feeling my feet hitting the ground, or my brain talking incessantly. The heaviness of my body was gone, much as when Tobe and I became blended energy the last night of his life.

Not long after this incident, I was turning off the outside faucet and for some reason, looked up at the grass and the barn beyond. I stood up and kept looking because again, that knowing absolutely, no question about it that the grass and barn and everything around me was something I had created from Thought, the work not of my mind, but my soul. I was not separate from them, nor them from me – they were a reflection of who I am. And then, all appeared normal again. Although increasingly I find it difficult to define what 'normal' is! Is anything truly what it appears in this reality, to be? Certainly, it is a wild and wonderful adventure to encounter other possibilities and realities.

Sam, a magnificent collie/shepherd was a fiercely loyal companion of mine many years ago. He came to me and my family when he was 6 months old, a battered, frightened pup, and stayed by my side for 15 years. He was one of the most remarkable dogs – and beings – to ever grace my life.

Sam was far more intelligent than I ever could be; his intuitive sense was razor sharp, he "read" people and knew friend from enemy and was not the least reluctant to protect me from all possible harm. Yet he also loved and respected my friends and family. Once, my friend, Mary (who holds only the highest respect for all creatures) was sitting across from Sam as I made coffee in the kitchen. When I returned to the living room she remarked with awe, "He is *not* a dog!" His piercing gaze met with hers in a most profound way. He saw in her a remarkably loving being and they connected on that common, mutually respectful, sacred ground.

Light met light. It was that simple. At the time I could not explain their interaction so simply or quickly, but years of delving into matters of quantum physics and consciousness brings me to such a point.

You see, while atoms are the basic building blocks of all physical matter (including air, Sam, myself and Mary) they are far from the smallest of the composite of all things. For instance, within each and every atom is a photon, or particle of light. The chair you may be sitting on right now contains billions of particles of light. The cup you drink from, composed of atoms, contains particles of light. Even the tick or spider we try so hard to avoid, is composed of atoms and thus, particles of light. And while this is scientific fact that by itself might not impress many people (unless they are physicists, or like me are hopelessly curious about how things work) every so often even the most distracted person will suddenly find themselves drawn to another being, even place, by a remarkable connection they cannot really explain. Between people it might be a friendship or love at first sight. But what about the sunset that stops you in your tracks, or the single bird call that signals dawn, or the exquisitely deep purple morning glory blossom on the fence post?

And what of the dog who nestles next to you on the sofa, who looks to you with adoration and complete trust? Or the rescued cat who purrs and rubs against you, showing you his or her most sincere appreciation? What of the butterfly that lands on your outstretched hand and turns to look at you?

These are moments of awe, moments of absolute soul-synchronization.

Sam, and countless other beings of all species and kind (including mountains, trees and water) have, and always will, share with me that comradery of the heart – truly light given and light received in its physical nature: as particles and as waves. But what if unconditional *love* is the particle/wave physics, the photons of the soul? And what if they are one and the same?

How easy it is to overlook the ordinary until it catches our attention. The quartz rock on the sidewalk would remain unnoticed, but trip over it, and suddenly it becomes highly visible! Bend down and pick it up (no, don't throw it away in anger or otherwise treat it carelessly) and turn it carefully in your hand. Is it gold, white, or rose colored? Maybe a bit of each, colored veins shot through translucence as well. The edges are crisp, definite, not the soft, rounded ones of sandstone or limestone, that once formed beneath the sea. No, your personal tripping stone found its rocky birth in a bed of raging hot lava, spit forth from the heart of an erupting volcano. Was it enormous – bouldersized – when it began its travels down the volcano's side, or was it molten rock, flowing thick and glowing until the air or water (if it hit a river) caused it to congeal. And how many eons ago? Millions, perhaps billions of years ago? Look at the rock in your hand – it is already ancient and not yet done; in fact, it never will be "done" – because it will continue to wear down over time to sand, to dust, then become part of the soil's composition from which might spring an oak tree, plants or bushes, certainly be home to earthworms who turn and nourish the soil, and perhaps to a groundhog, mole, or vole who digs down and down to form a warm nest for its offspring. All this in a single stone. Whole scenarios and worlds opened to you because you stopped and really looked, first at the stone's physical composition, and then the history it carries in its form, past, present, and future. All its probabilities; some of its possibilities, such a range! And in your hand: a slice of its history, the moments when its life and yours interact and become one history.

But "history" as we think of it is not necessarily a series of linear, physical events. Woven throughout what we sense on the material level are an infinite number of other levels of existence outside the boundaries of space/time, alternate rates of vibration, or frequencies, much like radio/cell frequencies, or the far ends of the light spectrum, colors we cannot see, but exist nonetheless, or sounds such as those heard by dogs and other animals of keen hearing, but not audible to us humans. In fact, what and who exist beyond our current capability to comprehend is staggering, and awesome. And then, there are the guides and angels....

A Guide for Each of Us

On a summer's day, Sam and I walked the path through our little woods, Sam testing the air for new smells, I preoccupied in matters of the day. Sam noticed first, the buzzards circling overhead and sitting in trees just ahead of us. As we approached the fence line, we saw a small fawn lying on the ground. He still had his spots, and he was dead.

The buzzards, voicing their frustration by our presence, left as a dark cloud heading back to the west while I placed the fawn's body on softer ground, covered it with leaves and then large pieces of fallen pine limbs, a makeshift grave on land too full of tree roots to dig into, making my sadness for the fawn's loss of life even more intense.

Job finished, Sam and I sat on the ground next to the grave. I closed my eyes in prayer, wished the little being a safe journey into spirit and called upon the Light to surround and protect his spirit.

My head still bowed and eyes closed with tears pouring down my face, I was suddenly aware of motion to my right. It was as if I were watching the scene from a movie, it was so clear. The fawn's body was back where we had found it, and coming towards it was an enormous, pure white, shimmering stag, enormous antlers on his head, his feet moving as if on cushions of air. He did not seem aware of me or Sam, and my feeling was we were watching something that had already happened in time and space. The stag approached the fawn, and as he reached his great head down toward the body, the spirit/soul of the fawn rose fluidly from the lifeless body, moved beside the great stag, and together they turned and moved away, disappearing into a dimension I could not follow with my mind's sight.

I was stunned! I had witnessed a most profound event: the fawn had not died alone nor been left, in death, in a state of confusion, for a magnificent angel had come for him.

And so it seems those from beyond space/time enter our three-dimensional world to offer solace, love and peace, gifts from a realm that holds us all – every single being – in total, accepting, unconditional love. I want to assure you from my own experiences that what we call miracles occur constantly, all around us, for us. So many of those miracles are actually our own guides or angels (however you wish to call them) at work, watching over us, caring deeply about us. They are the most beautiful of blessings. While most go unnoticed, they come again and again without pause or restraint, ready for our acceptance. The light comes – sometimes in a shape we can relate to perhaps to ease any apprehension we might have at its presence because "it" wishes us no harm, quite the opposite. And sometimes, the light appears as just that, pure light.

When I was a child, I attended the birthday party of a classmate from school. After all the other children had gone home, I was invited to spend the night, an exciting prospect for me. But when bedtime came my friend's parents put me in a room by myself – it was dark and I was scared and homesick. I sat up in the bed, hugging my knees, sobbing. I just wanted to go home.

At the far end of the room a light appeared – bright but not blinding, no form to it, yet it was tall, steady, silent and still. I was not frightened of it, in fact, as I looked at that light, all my fear and homesickness melted away and I felt peaceful and calm. I lay back on the pillow and fell asleep for the rest of the night.

Back at home the next morning I went straight to my grandmother who I knew would trust what I had witnessed and explain the mysterious light to me. Without hesitation she said, "That was your guardian angel! Your angel is always with you, watching over you; don't ever forget it."

And I never have.

The white angelic stag who came for the fawn; the light that shone bright to calm my fears: miracles? Perhaps, but also there for every one of us, nothing and no one excluded, whether we chose to believe in them or not. A comforting thought in my opinion.

That Light which has returned in so many other ways and forms throughout the years and now seems more present than ever before. Angels, guides, ancestors, those who have gone on before, spirit animals, friends of the Light, ascended masters, God/Great Mystery/Essence: a great assemblage of love of the highest order.

A Different View

If I sit half way up the circular stairway in my living room, I see everything from a new perspective. As I move throughout the day and evening, most often I am looking at my surroundings at eye level, my mind scattered in many directions. And my surrounding are fine, lovely in fact, I live in a beautiful and peaceful place.

And when I climb the stairs some more and stop, turn and look down a different world opens before me. Inside, light streams in from the top of the windows because at this moment the sun has moved past noon and is just beginning its descent to the horizon. So it slants in, brushing along the very tops of the many plants and indoor trees. In various dog beds and on the couch, my elderly dogs sleep soundly, all three of them turned into little donuts, their bodies rising and falling softly with each breath. They and the furniture (dog beds included) all seem to be one mosaic from here, a tapestry of color, fur, breath and life. I look across the ceiling to the fieldstone fireplace and notice a tiny spider building her web, the normal movement of warm air rising gently, rocking it. Had I been standing on the floor, I would not have seen her. She joins the tapestry that spreads out beneath me.

From up here I can look out the many windows and glass doors in the living room to the front porch and even beyond the porch, to the small garden pond full of tadpoles and frogs, purple and gold Water Iris, thick green ferns along the pond's top bank, periwinkle flowing out across the side and down into the stone path that runs through the front garden. High in the Maple tree that stands just to the side of the pond is a crow, watching me. He turns his head this way and that; crows don't miss a thing. From where I sit, middle stair, we are on eye level.

If I go up just one step, everything changes. The living room becomes a bit smaller yet seems to spread out more. The porch appears more shaded, even more inviting on this hot, humid summer day. But best of all, now I can clearly see straight across the front garden, across the narrow road that runs in front of my house to the field on the other side. There, resting after a morning of grazing, are the neighbors' cattle, white, brown, gray, black – like confetti sprinkled in the grass. Some are asleep, their heads turned back on their shoulders; others are chewing cud, their heads forward, slightly extended. More peace; more of the tapestry that surrounds me – everywhere.

When I am out in the barn at night checking on the donkeys, what a different perspective there is outside engulfed in stillness, stars so bright, sometimes I just stand and try to count them. Impossible, of course, but intriguing. I am right up there among them! Back inside, I go back to bed and to sleep, carrying all the images with me. The tapestry continues to weave and spread out and wrap me in peace.

So easily I get entangled in the issues of my life, the obligations and demands, the worries and fears, deadlines and regrets. But if I stop, close my eyes, and climb the stairs in my mind, new vistas appear, peace returns, maybe for a short while, but it is enough. I am in the tree with the birds, or across the road, resting among the cows or curled on the couch next to a dog. Or by tucking all other images seen in daylight away into the equalizing power of the darkest night, I can count the stars. And most of all, so softly wrap myself in the tapestry of life. All it takes is a different perspective.

The same philosophy applies to the other realms and beings, unseen but ever present that join us in Life Unbounded. But so often I am too much in my head to remember them. And so I asked a question of the Universe (from which I have come to rely on and trust for guidance). And that question, simply stated, was (and remains) *How can I see this – Life – differently?*

Life-and-death situations with some of the animal members of my family brought me to ask such a question. Physical distress in ourselves is tough enough. The same in one we love is downright terrifying. It overwhelms, makes us feel helpless, as if what has gripped our beloved companion has power we cannot defeat. Well/ill; struggling to regain health/losing the battle. Here/gone. Gone where? Silence, absence? Yes…and no? Strong issues and questions that too often remain unanswered.

To hear the answer I sought, I had to go back to that fact that every single cell in every single being (even those considered to be inanimate) contains a photon or particle of light. And light doesn't become ill and die away, it shifts, actually expands, joins other photon particles – that's what I was shown when I asked my question, *How can I see this differently?* It's all about the light.

Life in all its stages is not about here versus not here, alive versus not alive, but about continual, uninterrupted transformation, going out, returning, every nano-second, life moving within itself to become ever more evolved, ever more *Alive* just on different planes of existence. But how could I see my cat succumbing to cancer as anything else but death approaching? I dreaded getting up in the morning to face another day of his decline. And so pushed by despair, I asked my question. And clear as anything in my mind I heard, "Look into his eyes." I did, and what I saw was clarity and a light so beautiful it made me weep. His true nature emerging, ready to move on out of his tired, ill body, ready to blend with the light that is everywhere, even into my own weary, grieving soul. And I remembered the stag who came to lead the fawn's spirit into the great Light, and the light at the end of the room when I was a child…how many times over my life have I met that light!

"Look to the light and you will find me there," my bovine friend, Christina had told me after she died. I did, and it worked, not that I saw her physical self, but a brightness that surpassed the small garden light I chose to look into. It wasn't the first time a magnificent light had appeared to me when someone I loved had crossed dimensions. I know, and I trust that light; it's already everywhere, it is part of all of us, me and you and those we share our lives with. But we need to turn our minds to the light and focus, focus, focus.

From a practical, deep in the throes of distress position, sometimes all we can do is *trust* in the presence of the light, and the best ways I have found to do this is to keep a candle burning (battery powered one is fine, too), sit in the sun for a while, or look at the moon. Acknowledge that light, even if you don't see it with your eyes or feel it with your heart. Talk to it, thank it for being with you, being an inseparable connection between you and the one who is ill. And don't forget to ask the Universe (or however you wish to call that great all-loving Energy) to help you eventually see things in a different and kinder-to-you, way.

Take Heart!

THE FIRST HEART TO SHOW up here was a large rock of sizeable weight, carried and placed at Michael's feet by Sunshine.

Sunshine, a Golden retriever who lived across the road, adored Michael who was then still in middle school, and would show up every day to play Fetch the Rock/Stick/Ball, whatever was at hand. Michael is not particularly a dog person, much preferring the company of cats. But for some reason known only to her Sunshine had chosen Michael to be her friend, in fact her best friend. She loved him. And, he loved her. So when she dropped a heart-shaped rock at his feet one morning, it was no surprise to any of us, certainly not to Sunshine.

Eventually, Sunshine left this world and Michael grew up. But at some point, several years ago, heart-shaped stones again began showing up here, just on their own. They would be tiny to large, on the ground, or propped against a tree. When more and more began appearing I collected them and brought them in, with the exception of a few who quite clearly let me know they preferred to just be left where I had found them.

Really? you ask. *How did you know?* I understand your skepticism, but while most of the stones sat easily in my hand, those few would roll off my hand back to the ground, or seem incredibly heavy for their size, or it just seemed the right thing to do to put them back. I began to understand the messages and to just trust my intuition regarding them.

Then other hearts began showing up. Something was afoot, someone was sending me a powerful message. I wasn't quite getting it, perhaps "We/I love you"? or "You need to be a more loving person", or "Love is what truly matters"...it's easy to get too involved in meaning and forget to just say Thank You and enjoy the gifts. For gifts they were.

When my mother died in early 1998 five of us held a small ceremony for her high up in the Blue Ridge Mountains, releasing her ashes into the wind. I threw handfuls of ashes while our friend, Jo took pictures (those were the days of film). I remember that the last handful of ashes I threw seemed to stay longer in the air than the previous ones. But then they dispersed in the wind, we all said a quiet prayer of thanks, and went back to the car.

The car we were in was, for a change, clean so it was a mystery how five shiny pennies were sitting together on the center console when we got back in. They had not been there on our trip up the mountain.

But I knew. Mom's spirit was there with us. When alive, she would often dig in her purse for change and hand me a shiny penny for good luck, and I would reciprocate if I found one in my wallet. It was our sign of affection for one another.

In time, Jo had the film she had taken, developed. The last picture is of me, arms wide, having just released that last handful of my mother's ashes... and indeed they did hang longer in the air, forming an enormous, perfect heart.

About a month after Mom died, I bought a new kitchen

stove. The first night it was installed a small saucepan slipped out of my hand and fell on the edge of the stove, chipping out a small piece of the white enamel. And the shape of the chip? A heart, of course. A week later I was cutting into a bud of garlic and in the center of the bud? Yes, a small and perfect heart.

The hearts kept coming – all sizes, some in the most unusual places. A drop of clear water on the stainless kitchen sink; a small piece of watermelon that slipped off the spoon onto the counter; a chunk of toast that fell onto my plate; a "scar" in the trunk of the Maple tree out back; a large splash of water from Christina's water bucket; clouds in the sky; dog or cat food scooped from a can, a piece of cheese, and always the parade of small heart-shaped stones silently calling to me as I crossed the yard or walked in the woods, or climbed the driveway from the mailbox by the road.

Too many hearts to ignore. Too obvious and too frequent to be called coincidental. Always a joy, always gratefully received.

I still find hearts – sometimes there are long stretches of time when none appear, but without fail one will show up when I am feeling sad or scared or confused. And sometimes, 'Just Because'. I don't ask questions, or question them anymore because I know:

Someone loves me!

The Power of Dreams

EVER SINCE CHILDHOOD, MY DREAMS have often been significant. I usually dream in vivid color, even remember odors, sounds and music after I have woken up. Even decades later some of my dreams are still clear to me.

My most important dreams I loosely refer to as my Teaching Dreams, because either they demonstrate something I need to know for my own spiritual growth or I need to put into practice. At the end of these kinds of dreams, I will receive a message, but from whom I do not know, yet the messages are always powerful, helpful and kind. Such dreams always come just before I wake in the morning and I have no trouble remembering every detail. I pay close attention to these kinds of dreams.

The first dream I remember with absolute clarity happened when I was quite small, maybe seven or eight years old. In my dream I can see myself, as that young child, coming out of a small cottage and walking down to a fast-running stream not too many yards away from the front door. The cottage is surrounded by tall pines, a dense and friendly forest. I am quite at home here. I seem to live alone and the cottage is my house.

As I stand by the stream, animals start coming out of the

forest to join me – deer, rabbits, birds, foxes – they are all my friends, my family. I could not be happier here.

And that is the end of the dream. I can easily recall the deep green of the pines and the translucent nature of the water and my delight for all the animals. Each time I think of this dream, I realize it defines who I was when I was born, and who I have been, in my heart, all my life, living with love for, and in harmony with all of nature. Sometimes the memory of this dream has been a lifeline when I have gone through difficult times and felt lost and unsure of myself. Along with the light I saw in the bedroom when I was young, it has been one of my greatest treasures.

Ancient of Friends

Another dream. There are several of us in a medium-sized room. I stand close up front, looking to the back of the room, as if this is a camera shot and I am holding the camera, the others, talking happily among themselves are further from me. I don't know the other people, but I recognize you, a tall man with dark, thick hair. You turn and look at me, leave the others and come to me. You take my face in your hands, looking into my eyes with such kindness and love. And in the wordless gesture is the assurance that even though I must be "here" (Earth, physical reality) and you must "there" (another vibration/dimension) you are always aware of me and always care for and about me. We are ancient friends, inseparable in spirit/soul. No other words are needed.

The dream ends, leaving me with a great sadness and longing.

We had met before in dreamstate, 20 or more years ago. What I still clearly recall is standing in front of you – you look quite stern, you are telling me I have to go back, I belong in my body in the physical world, but I don't want to go. I have never felt such love as we share – it is not of this world for sure.

Suddenly, I wake up. It is the middle of the night and tears are pouring down my face. I have never forgotten how I felt – the love, the grief for being torn away. Who are you?

A Guardian, a Desk; Reverence and Peace

In this dream, I stand in the upstairs bedroom of my current home, amidst stacks of packing boxes. Am I moving? It doesn't seem so, but looking around I notice all the furniture is gone. People roam noisily around the room and hallway, helping to pack. It's crowded and confusing and I am uncomfortable with it all. A friend of mine, who is a medical doctor, is there and says with urgency, "We have to go right now."

Then we are all standing on what seems to be a second-story stone terrace, part of a Benedictine monastery in a modern city. The monastery is very old, hundreds of years. My doctor friend tells me I have to get to the stone terrace below, but as we look over the wall it seems too far down with no apparent way to get there.

Suddenly I am over the wall, heading for the ground, but as if in slow motion – a feeling that I am being carried, rather than falling. Beside me, to my right, is a tiny pure white winged insect, a moth or butterfly. I land on the ground, my feet gently touching down and the white winged insect hovers near me. I look back up to where I had just been and it seems impossibly high up. How did I get down here without being injured or killed? The ground I stand on is paved with large, flat stones, well-worn by the feet of monks over the centuries.

And then somehow everyone who had been on the upper terrace is moving with me as we approach the ground floor entrance of the monastery. In front of us is an enormous door of ancient, hand-carved wood. The hinges are hand-forged iron, long and strong. As we enter what appears to be a smallish outer room, the Abbott comes through an inner door to greet us, but he looks displeased because the people with me are chattering loudly to each other, as tourists might, not the least respectful of the history or sanctity of where they are.

I, on the other hand, immediately feel so comfortable, a deep sense of humbleness and reverence for the place, from the stone floors to the walls of deeply stained oak. Despite the incessant talking around me, I experience great peace. It is almost as if I have walked back in time and the others were only memory. I know I had been a monk in at least one previous life and my love of God has always been very strong since childhood, but this is nearly overwhelming for me. I feel that I have come home.

I walk across the room, drawn to a small writing desk under a many-paned window that looks out and up to the inside edge of a sidewalk. We are, apparently, just below street level. I can feel the energy of the desk – it is so familiar to me, a very old friend one hundred or more years old and made from a strong wood. Its surface is mellow and smooth from the arms and hands of so many who have sat at it and written there, perhaps hand-illumined manuscripts or some other such religious documents. The front of the desk drops down with little cubbies and drawers built in and a hole for an ink well is on the top back ledge of the desk.

I hear a noise on the other side of the window and look up to see the feet and legs of two teenage girls walking past. They are laughing and drinking Slurpies from a local Seven-Eleven convenience store. What a contrast to what I am experiencing inside the room!

I turn back to all the people standing around talking way too loudly, to the annoyed Abbott, and then through them all weaves the little white, winged creature. But as it crosses the room it begins to lose its whiteness and transforms into a common house fly – and then it is gone.

And then the dream is gone and I am waking up. Since the dream, I have wanted to build that desk. I can still see it so clearly in my head, but don't know how to put it down on paper. I long for it.

As with many of my dreams, I clearly remember, years later every detail of it, one of those famous teaching dreams! So how to interpret this particular one?

Or was it *reminding* me that now, at this point in my life it is time to set aside all that I have thought to be important? First I was packing away what must have, at one time, had a reason for being in my life. Was I making room for what has always meant so much to me, my love of Spirit, simplicity and peace? A time of reverence and humility? In my "leap of faith" by way of a potentially dangerous descent back to "ground" I was reminded that I am always protected and carried by someone I was not aware of. I landed safely, accompanied on the journey by the winged insect, a visible reminder of that guardian. And furthermore, as I realized what was most important to me now, by then transforming into a house fly, the white winged being confirmed what I have always believed, that all beings, all things, contain that pure spirit. Thank goodness I had stopped killing flies years ago!

Surely my doctor friend represented the catalyst for my healing, by urging me on and to leap forward despite the apparent risk.

And the desk? I pondered on that one for weeks. Was I to find one just like it, or have it built? And then it occurred to me that perhaps it was telling me to write. And so, here I am.

A Dream of Louvered Doors

Another dream remains so clear. I know it is telling me something important:

I am talking to a man whose face I can't see as he has his back to me. He is grieving for the loss his dog. I say to him:

"Life – death – and *Life,* in all its fullness is like this: it's as if there is a pair of louvered doors between here, this world, and 'there', the next world."

And the visual that appears to us as he turns to face me are of two pure white louvered doors. The louvers serve two purposes. They let light (which represents soul and spirit) pass through from one side of the doors to the other. Their white color represents Spirit: The Whole/Holy. While they appear to be the partition between the worlds, they also serve to demonstrate how light from the other side always streams through to this side as well, thereby helping us understand we are never *dis*-connected or shut off from those who have crossed over.

When the doors open, a soul is leaving this world through them. Conversely, a soul is coming back into this world from the other side. All of this represents the fullness and interconnectedness of all life here and beyond here. The two doors meet in the middle. There is no latch or lock.

I understand all of this in the very instant I see the doors and the light streaming through the louvers.

Then I say to the man, "And dying is like standing on this side of the doors, pulling them open wide towards you, and stepping through and…" (as I point to the other side of the doors) "Look!"

And there for both of us to see is so very beautiful: Light, trees, mountains, ocean, sky, birds and other creatures – all of *LIFE* in brilliant colors and sounds, so much brighter and clearer than on this physical plane. And standing just on the other side of the doors is a dog, *his* dog looking at us, shining and beautiful; she is wagging her tail.

The man is laughing, tears streaming down his face, for this was – and – is, his companion.

"I know you can't wait to go right into it all," I say to him. "When it's time, you will feel such a rush of joy and laughter through your whole being. You will still be you, only in your Light body and it feels wonderful. And it's that way for everything that exists here and 'dies', including your friend."

The man steps forward as if he wants to join his companion, but the doors slowly close; it's not his time yet. He can still see her through the louvers; it seems to be enough for him for now.

"She'll be waiting for you," I say. He smiles and nods.

That was the end of the dream.

Interior Dreams

I. *Chaos*

Tim and I are standing in our house. I don't recognize it, but I know it *is* our home in this dream. It is a lovely, tidy and peaceful place, full of light, big windows and green plants, many with flowers. Tim is young, maybe ten years old.

We walk over to a door that leads to an interior closet. I recognize the closet from the house I actually grew up in Connecticut. Long and rectangular with shelves on either side, it used to hold all the games and toys my sister, Sylvia, and I had when we were young. But as I open the door to the one in my dream, it is full of stuff – all piled haphazardly, no longer toys and games, but old, unused things, pushed in for storage. At the other end of the closet is another door and because we are curious as to what is on the other side, we tidy the closet as best we can and step through it.

We open the other door and find it leads outdoors, but not to a garden or lawn as we had hoped. Instead, we, and the house, are standing on a tiny triangle of land in the midst of a large city, traffic whizzes past us on either side and it is noisy and cold with nothing but cars and trucks, buildings, pollution and concrete and asphalt.

Quickly we retreat inside, close the door, and go back through the closet into the peace of the house. It is undeniable which environment we both have chosen to live in.

II. *Tranquility*

A different dream. I am standing in front of the same closet; Tim is not with me this time, I am alone. I am once again drawn to open the door and step inside. But this time, with the closet now much tidier, I see that most of the floor is actually a trap door with a large metal ring for lifting it up. And I remember that the toy closet of my childhood did, indeed, have such a trap door. Beneath the closet floor was an old rickety wooden staircase that led to a cellar that was dark and musty, being several centuries old for the house in Connecticut that I grew up in had been built in the 1600s.

But in my dream I am able to easily lift the heavy trap door and descend the stairway, and as I go the stairs change from old wooden, dusty ones to lovely wide steps with fine wooden treads and open backs. The stairway makes a right-angle turn and I step onto a beautifully tiled floor next to a large built-in pool, lit from beneath the water and full of Koi fish.

As I look ahead I see a long wide hallway, bright and inviting. Again, the floor is clean and tiled. As I walk down the hallway, on either side I see four large rooms, two on the right and two on the left. And in each room, flooded with light is a very large rectangular shallow pool, full of iridescent, absolutely clear, shimmering water. An immense sense of tranquility is present and I want to stay here forever.

I know I have to return upstairs and I do so reluctantly, but even though I experienced these dreams over 20 years ago, they are strong in my mind, and the pools of water and their sense of peace remain with me. When I am feeling my life is out of control, I will often sit quietly and in my mind descend those stairs to revisit those pools of water. The positive effect is immediate.

I believe that both dreams demonstrated to me that in the outer, surface world, the world that seems so real, chaos and disorder are generally what I see and experience. But if I can clear a space within my own mind and "descend" into the interior of my true nature that is where I will find the tranquility and clarity that is always with me. I just have to be willing to do so. I feel this is true for everyone.

I usually fall into REM sleep very quickly when I go to bed at night. I've put in a long day, pushed my limits and I am ready to rest and repair. I always invoke the Archangels and other protectors to watch over and care for myself, my family, and all those I know. Often I am asleep before I can finish. But on rare occasions, just as I am entering that state between prayer and sleep, some sort of gateway seems to open, and words/thoughts will start pouring into my mind. I have learned to reach for the notebook and pen I keep beside the bed and write down as much as I can remember of what has been told to me. As I finish my notes and read them back, I am always astonished – and honored – to have received such wisdom. Once again I feel reassured that prayers as connections to those who care about and protect us, are real. So the following came to me as I was moving into that first deep sleep. No one announced him or herself as the author of the words, only that the words came imbued with a deep sense of respect and love for all of us.

The River of Knowledge

Knowledge is like a river. In early years knowledge moves swiftly, deftly, in narrow channels, skipping across the surface.

As one gets older knowledge slows, deepens, spreads out past the banks of its confinement. It is more open, tolerant, wider, more gentle.

And eventually as one approaches and crosses through "death", knowledge empties into the great ocean of All Known Things, one's own gathered knowledge throughout one's lifetime blends into *all* knowledge enhancing and enhanced by that great ocean of All Known Things.

When we are born, knowledge springs immediately into our brain, pouring in as from a fountainhead from our new, present world, still interblending with all the knowledge we bring in from the world we have just left.

In early years, knowledge of the old world becomes diluted by the ever-increasing rush of new knowledge and it carries us along, sometimes at dizzying speeds, in a head-long rush as we grow.

Eventually, into knowledge, like that aging river breaching its banks, wisdom starts to blend, and knowledge of the next world (which is also the world we left to be born here) begins to back-wash into our minds, knowledge and wisdom that is gentle, kind, and reassuring.

Tough Stuff

5:07 A.M. Thursday. I'm sitting up in bed writing down these words because they called me awake. From Whom? I have no idea! But the nudge to pay attention was strong and kind, as if from a caring friend, teacher or parent. I woke up with these words ringing firmly in my head, perhaps from my grandmother Elsie (who I know watches over me), the words so reminiscent of her poem, "Assurance":

"I have thoughts for you."

And here is what followed:

We're tougher than we think we are – after all, we are made of the stuff of stars. We fall down, but somehow we get back up again. We may fail at one endeavor but we turn and try another.

No matter how strong the storms of life twist us around, there is always that part of us, in our deepest, most beautiful core that will not give up. It is the eye of our personal and global storm, the still point that resides deep in the heart, individually and cosmically.

And it may not be right now that we eventually succeed, or next week, or it may not even be until February, but at some time, it's all going to be all right.

More About the Spirits
of the Tree People

MY HOME IS FILLED WITH trees - mostly the indoor variety, ficus and schefflera, but my little "forest" also includes two avocado trees and two robust corn plants. Everyone has reached ceiling height and have sturdy trunks; they have a definite presence here and I adore them.

I admit to hugging trees – something about wrapping my arms around one of the great Virginia pines that live in my *outside* forest is comforting. And then there is the one that has been growing at a nearly 45 degree angle. When I am bent over in arthritis pain it inspires me, to keep on going, and I thank her (she has cones) for that. I will often stand beside the pines and Maples and, lifting my head high to gaze at their magnificent crown, wish them a good morning, or safety in a coming storm.

And four times they have answered me.

The first time actually involved the entire row of trees – pines, oaks, dogwoods, and locusts that line the top of the property above the road. I noticed one day that they were all shaking as if being blown by a strong wind. Yet, there was no wind and all the other trees on the property were still. It did not take me long to understand what was occurring. Across the road, on a property of hundreds of forested acres that rise up into the Blue Ridge Mountains, loggers were clear-cutting without being selective, as is the more responsible way of thinning a forest. Enormous machines were simply ripping up and throwing down everything in their path, from new sprouts to old growth trees. It was a painful sight for me. But that day, it was more – I realized "my" trees were frightened by what they sensed – would they be next? Did they feel the pain and fear of their fellow trees across the road? And so, they shook.

I walked down the line carefully touching each one, speaking softly to them reassuring them they were safe. They were on my property, no one would be cutting them down. By the time I had walked the entire row, they had all stopped shaking.

My writing desk stands in the living room by a window that faces my little 2-acre forest where my goats and donkeys foraged. I loved looking out that window to see them, and I became very fond of one particular pine tree that seemed to have real character, a bit lopsided, but tall and lovely none-the-less. I would greet that tree through the window and hoped we were friends.

The second time a tree communicated with me was during the year the pine bark beetle came through this part of Virginia, decimating the forests. A few of my trees were attacked, but not all. However, I noticed the needles of my favorite pine were turning an alarming brown and I worried endlessly; it simply could not die.

But obviously it was in trouble. Eventually all of the needles had turned brown and were falling off, except for one bright green sprig about half way up. As had become my daily habit, I went out and stood beside the tree, placed my hand on the trunk, and prayed for a miracle. But this day tears poured down my face; I was losing my friend. Suddenly I felt a light pressure on the top of my head. It was so evident, I looked up to see who had put their hand there. But of course, there was no one and I realized it was the spirit of the tree trying to comfort me. The next day the green sprig was gone as well, but I knew the spirit of the tree was now free and that yes, indeed, we had and always would be friends.

When I walk the dogs in the forest I often stop to look up at the tops of the trees admiring them. One day, as I stood next to one of the larger of the old pine trees, suddenly I stepped out of physical reality and I "became" the top of the tree, looking down at this very small human being who was looking up at me! There was a sense of curiosity and affection and while this lasted only a few seconds, since that encounter I know that the trees are as much aware of us, as we are of them. I feel they respect and love us as well without expectation or judgment.

One summer evening I stood by the Maple tree by the back door. The light from the kitchen illuminated the branches and leaves; it was all so beautiful. A small branch that reached very low, all of a sudden eased over a few inches and carefully laid its leaves against my cheek. No other branches or leaves on the tree moved, there was no wind. Not even a breeze. I didn't dare move. The branch kept the leaves against my face for 15 seconds or more, but who could count during such an incredible experience? And then the branch moved slowly back to where it had been before. Without the need for words, the tree and I cared for each other, as we continue to do today.

It's Not as Empty
as You Think it is

ONE MORNING WHEN I OPENED my email; there was a new message from my friend, Elizabeth. Her mom, she said, had passed peacefully the night before, following a stroke and failed heart. "I will miss her all the rest of my life," Elizabeth wrote.

I closed the computer screen and bowed my head. My intention was to send prayerful energy to Elizabeth and her family. Instead, her mom came right to mind. I had not known Elizabeth's mom, yet there was a palpable energy all around me, sweet, vibrant, glowing energy. The energy's presence "spoke" of being well, whole and completely joyous. I knew that the energy was that of Elizabeth's mom visiting me as I sat there thinking of her, my friend, and her family. Did she want me to tell her daughter what I sensed? I knew I would. My friend and I share a love of, and strong belief in all kinds of angels and spirit guides and certainly her mom qualified as one.

As the sensation around me faded I realized how many others had come to me right after their crossing out of this world. Until I really thought about it, I had no idea how many times I had been visited. Each one, in their own way, human or animal, had eased, just enough, that great gaping hole left behind when someone dies. Into that silence, what I had always felt to be empty space, poured their true essence, the soul and spirit they always have been and always will be.

Those who have come to me after crossing the threshold out of the physical world, as that pure, joyous, energy are just as real, just as vital now, and just as present. When I can clear my mind of everything, including grief, even for the briefest of moments, I can intuitively sense them and know they have, in actuality, never left. So it really isn't empty here after all.

What We Are, is Light
(Yes, more about light,
it's that important!)

WELL, NOT ONLY LIGHT, BECAUSE certainly we are also matter and emotion and mental activity. But when it comes down to the basics, we are, apparently, simply light.

So how do I know this? Once again, a time of intensity brought illumination for me when it was the last thing I expected. Here's what happened.

Lyme Disease is deeply entrenched in my body and it is, on most days and even nights, a really tough journey for me. My Irish and Welsh heritage makes me stubborn enough to keep pushing forward and I admit to becoming stronger and more resilient the harder I push myself. But sometimes, especially by late evening, I've just had it.

And it was so, on one particular night, as I finally put my head to pillow after a long day of fighting immense fatigue and pain. As is my practice, I began my dedication for all beings who are suffering, sending blessings and prayers out across the cosmos. And then I began to fall apart. I called upon The Light – some would call this God, or the Christ Light, or Buddha – whatever or

Whoever inspires us. I needed help; I wanted to be cured. And as I called out for the Light to heal me, words swiftly filled my mind:

You ARE the Light! I heard. But I was not convinced. No, I wanted the Light to fix me! So I said aloud to the dark night:

If that is true, why then am I in so much pain?

More words flowed in: *Because you see yourself as separate, not only from everyone and everything else, but from the Light you call upon. And all beings – everything – are the Light. There is no place the Light begins or ends, no place it stands apart from you or anything else. You just need to accept this. That is all.*

And that really was all! No more words in my head even though I had more questions and still wanted a quick fix. But then I fell into a deep and restful sleep and didn't wake until morning.

I still have pain and fatigue, but my attitude towards it has changed. I am fighting it less, working with rather than against it. And that helps. As for recognizing myself as the Light, that's a bit harder. But if I take moments here and there to sit quietly, try to clear my mind of all its rampaging thoughts and worries and visualize myself standing in the midst of brilliant light, inner calm returns. And then I let myself flow into that calmness. It must be helping because I seem to be complaining less and appreciating everything more.

Wise One

TRUST ME WHEN I SAY one never knows when Universal wisdom will suddenly appear.

Late afternoon and a Master Soul was suddenly standing on my front lawn. I saw him through the glass doors of the kitchen sunroom, and when I stepped outside to better see him he raised his head and looked straight into my eyes.

His gaze was strong, steady, kind and piercing. I felt totally accepted and welcomed in his presence. On some level we were equals, perhaps by the great respect I held for him, and I sensed the same from him. Still, I was in awe of such a magnificent being.

No words were spoken, none were needed. He bent his head and continued the work he was there to do and I retreated quietly back inside. This great soul was embodied as the enormous and handsome bull who lives on the farm across the road. While my neighbors were away for the day, he had slipped through the fence and found his way to my small sanctuary and farm. A chance encounter? I have my doubts about that. After all, he could have wandered anywhere – further down the road, into another field, off into the mountain. But he didn't.

Two weeks previous we had met for the first time on his side of the fence when I was visiting my neighbor up at her house. He approached us as we talked, stood and looked intently at me, then laid down in the grass to continue watching me, unusual behavior for a bull! I was immediately captivated by his great and peaceful face and deeply intelligent eyes.

"He's very gentle," my neighbor told me; "he often stays to himself." Looking into his eyes, I was not surprised to hear this. And having shared 17 years with Christina, my own Hereford cow, I am well aware of the sentient nature of cattle. But bulls are often aggressive, being protective of their herd, and being so close could cause anyone alarm. Yet how intuitively comfortable I was with him; I could sit in the presence of this bull and never learn all that he could teach me. I was, with him, such a novice and not the least bit afraid.

As I watched him grazing on my lawn, I thought sadly that one day this magnificent being would most likely be sent to the stockyard, his ending in life harsh, painful and violent. But even before I could finish this dismal thought he looked up at me and in an instant I knew his response: That what lay before him was immaterial – to be bought, sold, even slaughtered was not why he was here, in this life, in this place, even in my front yard. What was to happen to him were almost imperceptible "blips" in the overall fullness of Life – before this lifetime as a bovine and well beyond it to what he would become again and again through time and space. He understood the totality of existence that is, was, and always will be, embedded within each of us, across all species, all beings. And it all was and would be nothing less than beautiful and perfect.

This wise one understood the *truth* of existence – a truth the majority of us once knew and will again, but for now have forgotten. And he had not.

Later that evening when it was nearly dark, my neighbors returned and came to lead him home. He went most willingly, following his kind "owners" and bucket of grain.

Even wise ones enjoy a good meal.

Compassion at a Concert

I WAS ENTHUSIASTIC ABOUT ATTENDING a concert given by two of my favorite musicians, R. Carlos Nakai and Peter Kater. The concert was in a small downtown theater, so I was not far from the stage where they would be playing.

Towards the end of the evening, Peter Kater played a piece he had written for piano, dedicated to Earth. The music was extraordinary and his love and respect for the planet was palpable. I thought to myself, *The Angels must really love this incredible artist.*

I had barely finished the last part of my thought when words poured rapidly into my mind, words I certainly did not expect. And they were:

Not only do we love this artist, but we love everyone equally no matter who they are.

There was a brief pause, then:

And you, too, dear one, can do the same.

And that was all — point taken! There was no sternness in the words that came, but I understood their importance. I have never forgotten the incident, or the lesson I was so generously given.

Bending Space and Time

I AM A NOVICE STUDENT of the science of physics and much of what I read I cannot get my brain to process, as it is usually presented in complex theories and wording. One almost has to be born a physicist to understand it! Yet it continually fascinates me, draws me back time and again. Perhaps this is because over my lifetime I have had experiences that simply cannot be defined in rational terms, events and encounters that do not fit into "normal" parameters of our known physical reality. Long ago I threw up my hands and declared, "Okay, whatever!" accepting them just as they presented themselves to me. And I am grateful for all of them, for to a one they have been helpful, positive ones, sometimes literally saving me from a certain death, or opening portals to other realms and the presence of the Beings of Light, my guardians and guides. Each event and experience strengthens my unshakable belief in those we may not always see or be aware of, but reside and operate side by side with us nonetheless.

When I started writing this book and as it has unfolded, I have realized that in every instance, in some way – small to boundless – there has been the hand of the so-called miraculous involved. With each step I take I have been shown how a mysterious and wonderful Energy has flowed through my life and all those I have come into contact with, from a single stone to the great Archangel Michael. And I capitalize the word Energy but it seems undefinable. Some call It God, or The Light, or the Great Mind, or the Tao – I will leave the definitions to you.

What follows are some specific examples of occurrences and encounters with the realm of the mysterious that stand out, for me, as extraordinary.

The Slotted Spoon Event

When clumping cat litter was first invented years ago, I would clean the cat box in my sunroom with a slotted kitchen spoon I kept hanging on a small hook, a thick piece of strong leather boot lace looped through the hole in the top of the spoon and knotted tightly together by which to hang the spoon on the hook. Every morning I would take the spoon down off the hook, clean the box, then hang the spoon back up again.

One morning when I took the spoon down, I found I was holding the spoon in my right hand and the leather boot lace in my left hand. *It must have broken,* I thought. I would have to find another leather lace. But then I noticed something odd. The lace I held in my left hand was not broken – in fact, it was still securely knotted together, forming an unbroken loop. *The handle (plastic) must have broken then,* I figured, that would make sense, right? But when I examined the handle of the spoon, it was completely intact, the plastic not broken at all, the hole in the middle of the handle as it should be.

I must have studied these two unbroken objects in my hands for some time. I was, quite naturally, confused, a bit dismayed because it did not make any sense, and spooked, because it was, well, spooky. Finally, I shrugged my shoulders and laid the leather lace aside. I would thread another through the unbroken hole later. One note of importance: the leather piece was old enough and tough enough as leather will get, that I was not able to untie it to reuse it. Eventually, I just threw it out.

Don't Sit Still!

Two events stand out for me regarding a process of time/the future that I have serious questions about. For example, when people ask me if I believe in reincarnation I always pause because according to Quantum Entanglement (again, by the most simplistic of my understanding of physics) in effect all time/event is simultaneous – past, present, and future co-exist, making all of our lifetimes concurrent. But this is a subject for a future book. Here, I mention Quantum Entanglement because I have, to date, had two direct experiences with the present and future meeting me at a single point in time. Both could also be considered as precognition, where unknown to me at the time of such an event, later in my life it would become my reality.

The first occurred when I was eight or nine years old, a happy child roller skating up and down the sidewalk in front of my grandmother's house in Connecticut, where I lived. Apparently, as I was skating, I thought to myself *I need to run and jump all I can because when I am older, I won't be able to use my legs.*

This would not be a typical thought of a happy child in the midst of playing! I probably forgot all about it in the next five minutes and might never have thought of it again. And I did go on in school to play field hockey, softball and basketball. I could run faster than most of my teammates, and for such a short person (barely 5 feet tall) I could jump so high, I made the varsity basketball team. I don't think I ever stopped moving fast no matter where I was going or what I was doing.

When I was in my 30s, I began to have some pain in my legs – mostly muscle pain, not enough to stop me in my busy lifestyle of raising my family and caring for the constant stream of animals in my small sanctuary. But one day while sitting in the sun, that childhood thought and image of me roller skating up and down the sidewalk, came flashing back to me. And there it was, that premonition, or as it turned out, precognition. For as the years have advanced, so has my difficulty with walking. I am no longer able to walk far, or climb hillsides or mountains without severe pain and fatigue, to the point that I wonder if one day I will be in a wheelchair as no medical cause or solution has yet been found, although the most likely cause is long-term Lyme Disease.

I go back, in meditation, to that first thought as a child and rewording and re-visualizing it, being grateful for my legs and recalling how they kept me mobile and without pain – rewriting the future? Or resetting what seemed destined to occur? If all is concurrent, why couldn't this actually happen? I don't have that answer, but I am still working at it.

And Don't Give Up

The second occurrence is a much happier one. In the summer of 1978 my family and I had decided to move from Massachusetts to Central Virginia. Our house was on the market and we were excited about our new adventure. But not all was going smoothly.

Our first visit to Charlottesville to look at properties was prompted by an offer on our house in Massachusetts. Arriving after a 12-hour drive with two very active small boys, we quickly discovered the only houses in our price range were small ranches in tightly packed communities. Our desire for an old farm house in the country with a couple of acres of land was, we were told by the realtor, impossible. "You are about two years late," she said rather impatiently. "Those no longer exist."

Despite looking at many properties with her, nothing appealed to us and we thought that perhaps our dream of moving South was unrealistic. At about the same time, the offer on our house fell through.

Back home we went. But a new offer was almost immediately presented for our house and we once again contemplated moving. But to where? To cheer myself up I began working on an embroidery piece I had bought some months ago. It was of a smallish two story house surrounded by gardens and a rock wall. When completed, the house would be yellow – my favorite color. I enjoyed working on it and decided I would make it into a pillow when done. I had no further thoughts on it.

The husband of our realtor in Charlottesville called to say a new property within our price range had just come on the market. So off we went again, two small boys in tow, 12 hours in the car, not very hopeful this time. I had just about completed my embroidery project and brought it with me.

The realtor took us 22 miles southwest of Charlottesville – way out into the country into the Blue Ridge Mountains to the small village of Batesville that consisted of several houses and old country story with a post office inside. Driving four miles south of the village we came to the property and as we drove up the driveway, I knew I was home. How could I not be? A small two-story farmhouse built in 1930 with a barn and chicken coup (with chickens) in back and almost three acres of land. A small forest sat within the property and across the road, a large cattle farm. Surrounding it rose the mountains, strong and serene.

But best of all? The house was yellow, my favorite color, with lots of gardens and a stone wall in front. I've been here nearly 40 years with no intention of moving.

I never found the time to make the embroidery piece into a pillow, but I keep it close at hand to remind me that miracles do, indeed exist, even without our asking.

What Friends are For

AN OLD FRIEND SHOWS UP in my life from time to time. We first met years ago, but I feel as if our companionship goes back forever and will undoubtedly continue beyond this physical reality. Sometimes, one just knows these things.

My friend, who wishes to be simply known as Sam (not his real name), somehow knows just when to knock on my door (so-to-speak), at a time when I could use some appropriate advice. A letter from him will arrive, often accompanied by a small present. Knowing that I, of stubborn Irish descent, am not especially good with receiving advice, this gentle soul lets me know that what he offers is no more or less than a gift presented with only the kindest intentions to be of assistance. Should I wish to receive his advice, he hopes I will re-gift it. And so I offer a small portion here. While there have been many more letters between us, the following are the most recent and basically sum up his consistent suggestions. I admit to finding them extremely helpful. Please feel free to re-gift as well. Sam would be pleased!

FRIEND OF MY HEART: HELLO again, and peace to you and all within your sphere of knowing: children, animals, friends and colleagues.

Do you remember, a year or so ago, my mentioning that

times and events would begin to fire up, get bent out of proportion, and cause quite a bit of chaos in the world? Well, here we are. Did you keep that letter I sent you? If not, I will, again, give you steps to take to help you navigate the difficult times.

First of all, turn off the news. At least, the greater portion of it. The news, while it informs, also fuels fear and fear only causes further imbalance, especially in one's health. Turn it off, walk outside, sit and listen to the birds and wind. Watch the sun cross the sky or the moon rise in the East. They have a lot to say that will help ground and encourage you.

Secondly, remember, as your Grandmother taught you, that you always have helpers of the "other" realms: angels, guides, old friends and of course, the ancestors. If their advice seems positive and loving, not only for yourself but for the Whole, act on it. That choice – to act – is yours alone. The "others" will not interfere or do your work for you. I've said this before, it's important to remember.

These "others" of the Non-Reality (Earth) are your best resource, that and the love you hold in your heart for all – everyone, no exception.

'Til soon again; your friend,

Sam

My Good Friend:

It's been awhile! Forgive my absence; the garden needed my attention, but you are never forgotten.

As said in my last letter, chaos does seem to be increasing in the world, but not without reason. From where I stand, humanity has made a mess of things and Earth is not so patient anymore. She stirs things up! I have to wonder how many of our (yours and my) kind are listening.

Knowing you, all that is happening is upsetting you. Your health is not so good, I hear. So at the risk of being forward, I offer, again steps to take to return you to a place of balance and joy. Let me know how you do.

Walk in peace.

Speak kindly, always.

Set anger and Judgment aside.

Offer a hand to others; give comfort by listening, but advise only as you are invited to do so.

Take no risks that would jeopardize your health or safety.

If you are tired, rest. Five or ten minutes will help tremendously. Try it and see!

Don't deny yourself a treat from time to time. See yourself as worthy because you are. *Do not put yourself last!* I am not implying that you neglect those around you or who are in your care, only include yourself in that circle of caring.

Give generously – not necessarily costly gifts or money itself if your own bank account is stretched, as I know it usually is. Some of the best gifts are prayer and blessing; love and encouragement. Small gifts are wonderful – a beautiful card, a pressed leaf of brilliant color (and as it is fall now, this a good time to stock up – I can send you some if you wish), a photograph that is awe-inspiring.

When confronted with anger or callousness, before responding ask your heart to help you find another way that sees with clarity and understanding. Why is that person wanting to cause you harm? What does that person need in his or her own life, causing pain and deflecting that pain onto you? The heart offers a broader vision, but how well I know how difficult it can be to not strike back. And, Irish that you are! But it is essential that you become the observer, not see yourself as a victim or target.

Peace is always within you, your constant companion, never diminished or absent. Peace is your core, your stillpoint.

And finally, dear friend, make clear choices you feel good about. Be grateful for everything in your life. And laugh! Find humor and joy, silliness is perfect. Just find delight every day as often as you can.

If you can do as many of the above suggestions as you can, I promise you *your* world will become so beautiful and strong and steady and full of meaning. And that you will take out into the world at large. Give it a try, will you?

Your friend and fellow gardener,

Sam

And in Conclusion:

The Third Grade Lunchbox Rescue – or,
Respect Goes a Long Way

BOTH MY SONS HAVE ALWAYS cared for animals. One night on his way home from work, Michael found a tiny injured kitten in the middle of the road and brought her home. I don't remember what number cat she became in our household, but we named her Gracie, a tough, vocal, determined-to-survive youngster who lived to be over 16. Thanks to Michael.

Gracie was closely followed by two kittens who were about to be drowned in a bag, again, rescued by my feline-loving Michael. Claire and Abigail stayed with us the rest of their lives as well.

Tim, his younger brother, extended his reverence for life to snakes, rodents and bugs. Now he is a dad himself and his son, at two years old, is showing clear signs of love for and gentleness towards animals. Both my sons are in their 40s with rescue and reverence still among their best qualities. I could not be more proud.

Back in 1983, the road I live on was much quieter than it is to-day. Three cars might drive down it in a day, rarely more. So my wanderlust dogs Sally, Sadie and Parsley ran free. And in summer, after a day in the fields and mountains, they arrived home cov-ered in ticks. I kept a small jar of kerosene on a windowsill of the back porch into which the ticks, carefully picked off one by one, would be deposited. It was the standard procedure in those days. It might be still; I would not know. Because:

In 1983, Tim was in third grade and not having his best school year. One day, after he departed the school bus, we sat on the back lawn discussing the troubles of being a right-brain dominant child in a left-brain dominant school system. Suddenly, Tim perked up and reached for his lunch box. Upon opening it, he searched inside, withdrawing something between his fingers.

"I found this by my desk today," he said proudly, showing me a tiny, very much alive tick. I was impressed; my son understood the importance of tick control.

I carefully took it from him, stood up and headed to the tick jar on the windowsill.

"What are you doing?" Tim yelled at me, rushing me with great indignation. "I didn't rescue it all day for you to kill it!"

I stared at him; I considered the tick squirming to get out from between my fingers; I looked again at Tim's confused expression. And I got it. I, who have rescued things including, yes, bugs and insects all my life, was about to commit murder in front of my son.

Together we walked the tick around to the front of the house and gently released it into the garden. It strode away happily, probably preparing to rush back around and hop on one of my dogs. But without any hesitation I knew I had done the right thing. All-grown-up-me had to be reminded about compassion for all life. Tim, all of nine years old, already knew.

An interesting footnote to this story which is, I promise you, absolutely true. Since that day of the Great Release, despite continued journeys into fields and mountains (even after we had to put fences up as the road traffic increased), rarely do I find a tick on any of my dogs. I find more on myself in a season than I have on all them. And, I have not killed any that I do find – ceremoniously recycled off the front porch, I am sure they bound off to find a likely meal, but at least not on my dogs.

Tim still had much to teach me. For it was not long after the lunch box rescue that we were inundated with flies. They tended to swarm in the spring and if I was quick enough, I closed up the house and they stayed out. But one day they beat me in. Up went the sticky fly paper in the kitchen and sure enough, the flies were drawn right to it. Can't have flies in the house, right?

Then down the stairs from his room came Tim, rescuer extraordinaire. Once again outraged over his mother's barbaric behavior, my angry child tore down the fly paper and proceeded to very carefully remove each stuck fly, washing their wings with a bit of damp tissue and releasing them back into the kitchen. Not a fly was killed or injured in the process and upon finishing the job, Tim defiantly wrapped up the now empty fly paper and threw it in the trash.

"Don't you ever…" he declared, glaring at me with those Irish eyes as he stomped back up to his room.

And since that day no fly paper has entered this house, not even a fly swatter. We have never had a swarm of flies again.

Have I really learned anything about being a kinder, more compassionate human being? I would hope so. It is my sincere intention that the book you hold in your hands speaks well of this. I know I came into this world to bring a message that has been vital to me for as long as I can remember, a message about the importance of what might sometimes seem to be an irrational, but necessary love for all beings: Love no matter what; love no matter why. Love just because it is the most pure and joyous healing energy there is. Snuggle close with a beloved dog and you will quite likely understand. But if you are open minded, you can find that love all around you.

Michael, Tim and I still put spiders, stink bugs and all manner of other small creatures outside rather than take away their lives as we continue to rescue dogs and cats in need of a family. And then there was that famous cow and the spotted rooster and the five stray ducks….After all, everyone wants and deserves to live, to thrive and to be content, don't they? Some ways to live with wisdom and compassion I brought in with me when I was born, we all do. And many more I have had to learn along the way with the help of so many fine guides and teachers from my children, my friends and other family members, to the many animals and all of the natural world. And of course I owe a deep bow of gratitude to my angels and guides of the spirit realms. For you all have shown me so clearly that we *can* find our peace and our joy, not just when the rain falls or the sun shines, but for all time.

Thank you to all within these pages, and so many more:

And in our footsteps, flowers grow

I follow your kindness
out into the world and
step by step by step
flowers grow where we
have walked.
Unfettered, they likewise
cast their seeds until
what remains before, behind,
around us
are endless fields
of grace and loveliness,
foundations for
a new and gentler world.

CPSIA information can be obtained
at www.ICGtesting.com
Printed in the USA
BVHW08s0724300818
525583BV00001B/1/P